17⁹⁵/

D0712817

HOW TO
WRITE & SELL

HOW TO
WRITE & SELL
TRUE CriME

How to spot local stories
and turn them into gripping
national bestsellers.

GARY PROVOST

Writer's
Digest
Books

Cincinnati, Ohio

How to Write and Sell True Crime. Copyright © 1991 by Gary Provost. Printed
and bound in the United States of America. All rights reserved. No part of this
book may be reproduced in any form or by any electronic or mechanical means
including information storage and retrieval systems without permission in writing
from the publisher, except by a reviewer, who may quote brief passages in a
review. Published by Writer's Digest Books, an imprint of F&W Publications, Inc.,
1507 Dana Avenue, Cincinnati, Ohio 45207. First edition.

95 94 93 92 91   5 4 3 2 1

Library of Congress Cataloging in Publication Data

Provost, Gary
   How to write and sell true crime / by Gary Provost.
      p.   cm.
   Includes index.
   ISBN 0-89879-446-3 (hrdcvr)
   1. Prose literature—Authorship. 2. Crime writing. 3. Crime—Research. 4. Non-
fiction novel—Technique.   I. Title.
PN3377.5.C75P76   1991   90-27596
808'.02—dc20   CIP

Edited by Nan Dibble
Designed by Sandy Conopeotis

FOR THEIR HELP AND SUPPORT
I WANT TO THANK

JOHN BRADY

BRIAN DEFIORE

NAN DIBBLE

KEN ENGLADE

JEAN FREDETTE

RUSS GALEN

TODD HARRIS

JACK OLSEN

CHARLES SPICER

AND

LISA WAGER

In October of 1988 three of the keenest minds of our time concocted The Bristol Plan, in Bristol, Connecticut. The plan is nothing less than a cure for almost all of society's ills. Since its most discussed feature is a complete overhaul of the criminal justice system in America, I thought it appropriate to mention it here. Because of their wisdom, their compassion, and their unquenchable thirst for justice, this book is dedicated to —

Frank Strunk and Keith Wilson

About the Author

Gary Provost is the author of eighteen fiction and nonfiction books, including *Fatal Dosage: The True Story of a Nurse on Trial for Murder*; *Without Mercy: A True Story of Obsession and Murder Under the Influence*; and *Make Your Words Work*. He has written thousands of stories, articles and columns for national, regional and local publications; humorous columns for more than 100 newspapers; and celebrity profiles for a dozen magazines. He is a popular speaker around the country and also conducts several writing seminars and workshops a year. He lives in Massachusetts.

TABLE OF CONTENTS

INTRODUCTION

A week before Christmas 1982, I got a phone call from Pat Piscitelli, an attorney in my home state of Massachusetts. He had gotten my name from a mutual friend. Piscitelli had been the lawyer for Anne Capute, a nurse who, in 1980, had been accused of deliberately overdosing a patient with morphine, and had been tried for first-degree murder. The case had gotten reams of local publicity and a fair amount of national notice, so attorney Piscitelli was confident that someone would publish a book about it. He wanted me to write that book.

At the time I was something less than the perfect person to write a true crime book. I had written books for children, books for writers, and a romance. I had also published about a thousand shorter pieces — articles, columns and stories. I had written about roller skating, glass painting, music making and igloo building, but not a word about criminals, police, courts, trials, lawyers, prisons, convicts, violence or bloodshed.

So I did the only sensible thing — I agreed to write the book. I reasoned that nobody has experience at anything until he does it for the first time. And, more to the point, I've always felt that a good writer can write well about anything that excites him. And I had gotten excited when Piscitelli told me about the Capute case. I saw that it had many of the elements of a compelling novel. There was a sympathetic central character in Anne, the lowly LPN who was being crucified by the hospital and the legal establishment. There was a knight in shining armor, in Piscitelli, the well-known lawyer who embraced the case even though Anne couldn't possibly pay his fee. There was formidable opposition in the cool and competent nursing supervisor who accused Anne; and in the cunning and ambitious district attorney who prosecuted her. There was domestic strife because Anne's husband was less supportive than she would have liked, and Anne's teenaged daughters were emotionally wounded in the crossfire of publicity about their mother, "the murderer." There were side stories, like the friend who shot himself dead in Anne's house during the trial while Anne's daughter slept in another room. And there was a happy ending, because Anne was acquitted of the charges.

1

Okay, so I had never written a true crime before. It didn't matter. I recognized a good story when I saw one.

So I wrote the book, *Fatal Dosage*, and it was published by Bantam Books in 1985. Later, I sold the movie rights to a producer named Jack Farren, and in October 1988, I was able to gather with fifty friends and, for the first time, watch something I'd written come to life on the screen. My book had become the CBS television movie, *Fatal Judgment*, starring Patty Duke and Tom Conti. Without any special training in true crime writing I had become a true crime writer.

I hadn't switched careers. And I hadn't abandoned the other kinds of writing that I love. Since *Fatal Dosage* I have written more children's books, more books for writers, a sports book, and more magazine articles.

But I have also written three more true crime books, and I'll give you a quick rundown on them, as well as my current true crime project, now, because I'll be referring to them often in this book.

Finder: The True Story of a Private Investigator (with Marilyn Greene, Crown hardcover, 1988; Pocket Books softcover, 1990) is the true story of Marilyn Greene of Schenectady, New York, a private eye who specializes in missing persons cases. In fact, she is the nation's leading finder of missing persons. I wrote this book about her career and her life in the first person, from Marilyn's point of view. Ninety percent of my research for the book was interviews with Marilyn Greene.

Across the Border: The True Story of the Satanic Cult Killings in Matamoros, Mexico (Pocket Books softcover, 1989) begins with the disappearance of Mark Kilroy. Mark was a college student on spring break in Brownsville, Texas. He went to Matamoros, Mexico, across the border, where he was kidnapped, ritually murdered, and mutilated by a satanic drug cult led by Adolfo Constanzo. When Mark's body was discovered, so were the bodies of twelve other victims. My book covers the investigation.

Without Mercy: The True Story of the First Woman From South Florida to Be Sentenced to the Electric Chair (Pocket, 1990) is the story of Dee Casteel. Dee, an alcoholic who was regarded by some as "the nicest person you could ever want to meet," worked as a waitress at a south Florida pancake house. She helped arrange for the murder of the restaurant's owner and his mother. For this, she and three men were sentenced to die in the electric chair.

The book I am currently working on under contract to Pocket Books is tentatively titled *Deadly Secrets*. It is a story about a well-liked and respected Florida man who tried several times to have his wife killed, and ended up killing the hit man he had hired. Beyond that, this man was leading a bizarre double life which included affairs, buying counterfeit money, destroying cars for insurance money, an obsession with guns, torturing people on film, and videotaping the murder of one of his employees.

Redbook bought first serial rights to *Finder*, and *The Star* bought second serial rights. Warner Brothers bought an option on dramatic rights. Pocket Books bought reprint rights. *Across the Border* had a first printing of three hundred thousand copies. *Without Mercy* has been published in both hardcover and paperback, as *Deadly Secrets* will be. And *Without Mercy* has also been optioned for a movie.

True crime, as you can see, has been good to me. It has given me more money than any other kind of writing. It has given me the chance to do the kind of writing I want—stories about interesting people in dramatic situations. And it has raised my name in the publishing industry so that I can more easily sell the other books I write.

And one other thing. Recently, I was prattling on to my wife, Gail, about my lifelong fantasy of being a private detective. "I always wanted to be the guy who comes into a strange town and snoops around," I said. "You know, like in the movies, find some waitress who 'knows something' and ask her questions, then talk to a cabdriver and drop in on the local police detective. Put all the clues together, then leave town and go on to the next case."

My wife looked at me for a moment, and smiled. "Gary," she said, "that *is* what you do."

Of course! Gail, as usual, was right. Writing true crime books had not just brought many of my writing dreams to life. It had also made my private-detective fantasies come true, and I didn't even have to get shot at. (At least, not yet.) Maybe I hadn't simply stumbled into the true crime writing field, after all. Maybe, wily detective that I am, I had known all along just what I was doing. In any case, deciding to write the story of Anne Capute was the smartest thing I've ever done in my writing career.

But this book is not about my career; it's about yours. You've picked up this book, and since it is unlikely that you mistakenly thought it was a book on how to smelt copper or the like, you must at least suspect that you are capable of writing readable true crime stories and that writing true crimes is right for you. Well, it *is* if you are interested in writing both fiction and nonfiction, because you'll need the doggedness of a journalist and the talent of a novelist. It *is*,

3

if you are fascinated by people who do the unexpected, places that produce the unlikely, and conflicts that pull like a magnet on all who come near. It *is*, if you can tell the truth even when the truth is not as interesting or as exciting as you had hoped it would be.

But if writing true crimes is not for you, it would be nice to find out now, so that you can donate this book to the public library and go bowling. Writing true crime *is not* for you if you are intimidated by authority, if you can't stand the company of lawyers, or if you cannot see the humanity in even the most violent and remorseless of criminals. It *is not* for you if you are bored by asking the same questions of several people, if you are horrified by the idea of reading twenty volumes of trial transcript, or if you get claustrophobic in prisons. And it *is especially not* for you if you are extremely uncomfortable in the presence of people who have suffered great pain. Make no mistake, when you write true crimes you are going to meet people who have suffered something awful.

Okay, so now that we've gotten that straightened out, let's move forward.

1

DEFINING THE
TRUE CRIME STORY

THE FATHER OF THE MODERN TRUE CRIME

n November 16, 1959 Truman Capote, then a well established
and much celebrated fiction writer who had turned increasingly to journalism, was intrigued by a small story on page
thirty-nine of the *New York Times*. It was a story about a
wealthy Kansas farmer, Herb Clutter, who had been murdered
in his home along with his wife and two kids. The family members had been
tied up and shotgunned in the middle of the night.

Capote was inspired to drive to Kansas where he intended only
to write a magazine article for *The New Yorker* about how such a
brutal murder affects a community. But this story swept into his life as
suddenly as any tornado surging across those midwestern plains, and
he was caught up in it, almost, it seemed, against his will. For the next
several years Capote could think of little else.

In 1966 Random House published the fruits of Capote's obsession, the book called *In Cold Blood*. It became the most discussed book
of our time. Capote's 384-page story about the murder of the Clutter
family in Kansas, the investigation that followed, and the arrest, trial,
imprisonment and execution of the killers, Dick Hickock and Perry
Smith, brought attention to the publishing industry that has never been
equalled, unless you count the *Satanic Verses* controversy of 1989,
which was really about censorship, not about a book.

Gerald Clarke in his impressive biography, *Capote* (Simon and
Schuster, 1988), writes:

When the book was published in January, 1966, the modern
media machine—magazines, newspapers, television and radio—became a giant band that played only one tune: Truman Capote. He was
the subject of twelve articles in national magazines, two half hour

5

television programs, and an unparalleled number of radio shows and newspaper stories. His face looked out from the covers of *Newsweek*, *Saturday Review*, *Book Week* and the *New York Times Book Review*, which gave him the longest interview in its history. *Life* ran eighteen pages, the most space it had ever given a professional writer, and advertised its huge spread by continuously flashing the words *In Cold Blood* on the electronic billboard in Times Square. "Such a deluge of words and pictures has never before been poured out over a book," observed a somewhat dazed-sounding reporter for the *New York Times*.

When *In Cold Blood* came out I was twenty-two years old. I inhabited a one room apartment in Manhattan, and I earned my living—forty-five dollars a week—by running errands for a watch company. I was a struggling writer who had not published a word. Though it had not occurred to me to write a true crime book, and would not for another sixteen years, I was thrilled by the attention Capote got for his book. I saw myself as a writer and he was one of "Us." I remember staring dreamily at the tall stacks of *In Cold Blood* piled in the windows of bookstores along Fifth Avenue. My heart beat faster just because an author was finally getting as much attention as a movie star or an all-star third baseman. And when I saw that one national magazine had Capote's picture on the cover along with the bold headline, "Death Spurns a Masterpiece," I was beside myself, not with envy, but with hope. It seemed to me that I had witnessed the ultimate dream of an author coming true. What could be better than to have a national magazine put you on the cover and say that your book is a masterpiece? Capote's success strengthened my resolve to become a writer.

During this publicity blitz a good deal was written about the form of the book. Capote was a master of self promotion, and he insisted that he had done something entirely unique. He brought a new term, "nonfiction novel," into the literary lexicon, and he was fond of telling the press that he had invented a new art form. In fact, he hadn't. The telling of true stories in fictional ways is certainly as old as story telling itself. While the term "nonfiction novel" is sometimes useful, it is never really correct. Capote's biographer, Clarke, writes:

In Cold Blood was a remarkable book, but it is not a new art form. . . . Indeed, the term he coined, nonfiction novel, makes no sense. A novel, according to the dictionary definition, is a fictitious prose narrative of considerable length: If a narrative is nonfiction, it is not a novel; if it is a novel, it is not nonfiction.

Clarke's criticism nonetheless, Capote had written an excellent book, arguably the best true crime ever written. If he hadn't invented the technique of writing a true story as if it were a novel, he was at least its best known practitioner and most enthusiastic promoter. His book brought more attention to the true crime book than any other. Because it was masterfully written, and because he chose to do it at all, the true crime book was elevated to the level of literature.

WHAT IS A TRUE CRIME BOOK?

So *In Cold Blood* is what we mean when we say a true crime book. We also mean *Helter Skelter, The Stranger Beside Me, Bad Blood, The Boston Strangler, The Hillside Strangler, Son, Nutcracker, At Mother's Request,* and *Fatal Vision,* to name just a few of the best known ones. There are hundreds more, because true crime has long been one of the most popular types of book. In fact, as I write this we are in the midst of a true crime boom. *Bitter Blood* by Jerry Bledsoe and *Small Sacrifices* by Ann Rule have only recently departed from the best-seller lists, each after residing there for many months. The same can be said for *The Mormon Murders* by Steven Naifeh and Gregory White Smith, *Blind Faith* by Joe McGinniss, *Perfect Victim* by Christine McGuire and Carla Norton, and *Missing Beauty* by Teresa Carpenter. My own book, *Without Mercy,* has been on some regional best-seller lists and has been featured on several national television programs. *Small Sacrifices* and *Blind Faith* have been television movies in the past season, and I'm sure that some of the others will be showing up on the tube.

"We're going through a huge surge in the popularity of the true crime book, both paperback and hardcover, right now," said Charles Spicer of St. Martin's Press, one of the editors I interviewed for this book. Other editors agreed. They also agreed with Spicer's prediction that, "Like any other boom, there will be a winnowing out process."

So maybe when you read this book true crime books will still be as fabulously popular as they are right now, or maybe they won't. But some high level of popularity is assured. The enormous audience for good true crime books and stories may shrink and swell over the years like the audience for any kind of book, but it has remained large and enthusiastic for decades and will continue that way for a long time. That audience of readers will welcome you with open arms and they will gladly pay the price of a book if you can write one that is exciting, compelling, fascinating and frightening. In order to do that, of course, you first need to know just what a true crime book is.

The term "true crime" represents a genre in publishing. That is, it's a type of book. Romance is a genre. Thriller is a genre. Private detective is a genre. These genres are labels that are put on books so that the publisher can assess and target the audience. When the publisher's salesman or saleswoman goes into a bookstore he can say "*Fatal Rain* is a new true crime by Scooter McElroy," which tells the bookstore owner a lot more about the potential sales than, "*Fatal Rain* is a new book by Scooter McElroy."

Obviously, the content of a book is going to be the prime indicator of what genre it is. A story about mice who can fly is never going to be mistaken for a political thriller. But since books don't always fall neatly into a category, the publishers have to do a bit of arbitrary defining. So, to a certain extent, a book is whatever genre the publisher says it is. A novel about a young man who solves his father's murder, for example, might be a mystery to one publisher, a psychological novel to another, and a young adult novel to a third.

What all this means to you is that not all books that are true and have crime in them are "true crimes" to the publisher. And if a book is not regarded as a true crime, then the publisher can't assume that it will appeal to that vast true crime audience. Thus, he might not buy your book, or might not offer you as much money for it as he would for a true crime.

So you can see where it would be handy for you to know what a publisher means when he says "true crime." Don't despair, I've looked into that for you.

I've talked to several editors about this and, not surprisingly, they all agreed that *All the President's Men*, for example, was certainly not a true crime book, even though it was true and was, to a large extent, about some crimes. They also agreed that a book about a Mafia hit man would not be a true crime.

"That," says Charles Spicer, "would be a 'mafia book,' a separate genre."

My own book *Finder: The True Story of a Private Detective* deals with a good many crimes, but it is not really considered to be a true crime book. It is the biography of Marilyn Greene, the woman who finds missing people, and it is usually placed in the biography section in bookstores.

So not all books that are true and about crimes are necessarily part of the genre called "True Crime." Then what is it that makes a book a true crime?

Charles Spicer at St. Martin's says, "I define a true crime book as one involving a murder. It's not about art theft, it's not about governmental cover-up. It's really a case involving a murder in which there's an investigation and usually a trial." Spicer says that among his favorite true crimes are Joe McGinniss's *Blind Faith* and Linda Wolfe's *Wasted*.

"I'm looking for a true crime where there's a story," he says. "I'm looking for something that's not just a magazine piece. If somebody just goes up to West Forty-Second Street and shoots somebody, that's not really the stuff of a book. There just isn't enough there. You have to have layers. The best of the true crimes give you some insight into characters, usually the character of the killer, and the situation that produced the crime. I'm doing a book right now about a woman from a well-to-do Virginia family who murdered her parents. The author dug into the past of the family and that of the girl and the result is that while we may not sympathize with her we have an understanding that we didn't have before."

Spicer, like all the editors I quote in this book, reads dozens of true crime proposals and manuscripts every year. He buys and publishes several, and he also reads the true crimes of other publishers to keep up with the field.

Another editor I spoke to is a woman at Putnam who we will call Betsy, because she does not want her real name used. Putnam, like St. Martin's Press, is one of the top publishers of true crime books. Betsy says, "To me a true crime is the nonfiction equivalent of a mystery. It has interesting people involved and there's a good investigation." Her favorite true crime is *Blood Will Tell* by Gary Cartwright, which she says is "one of the best true crime books ever written."

"Cartwright's book is great," Betsy says, "because he spends sixty pages setting the scene in Texas and explaining what Texas is and what Fort Worth is and who these people are. A sense of place is a very big factor in that book. I think if your book takes place in a great place and you evoke it well, it helps a lot."

And at Dell, senior editor Brian DeFiore told me, "I don't think a true crime has to have a murder. But it has to have an illegal act, and victims, and it needs some sort of investigation that brings the criminal to justice." DeFiore is an editor both for paperback reprints and hardcover and softcover original true crimes. One of his reprints, the best-seller *Perfect Victim*, is a good example of a true crime that has no murder. (It is the story of a woman who went hitchhiking one day in 1977 and was kidnapped by a man who kept her prisoner in a coffinlike box under his bed for seven years.) DeFiore's idea of a great true crime book? *Fatal Vision* by Joe McGinniss and *Blood and Money* by Thomas Thompson.

"I like to see real psychological insight into a character, both of the victim and of the criminal. I like to see real in-depth research into the place where the crime happened. A strong sense of place is important so that the reader can almost understand how such a crime could happen in such a place."

In an article in *Publisher's Weekly* Carolyn Reidy, president of Avon books, noted what she saw as three themes common in true crime books:

1. There are murderers among us.
2. Money can't hide evil or buy happiness.
3. Do I have the potential for this evil in me too?

To that she adds, "People these days feel threatened by their perception of increasing violence all around. There is both a desire to understand and a vicarious thrill in reading about violence."

WHAT DOES ALLAN SAY?

The publishing industry is notoriously unsophisticated about market research. There are no reliable surveys on just who buys and reads true crimes, and no one really knows if the audience is predominantly male or female, young or old, or anything else. We know which books have sold well, but beyond that we don't really know what the readers like and what they hate. So in the absence of a survey of thousands, I have conducted my own survey of one: Allan Provost, who, as it happens, is my brother.

Allan is an avid reader of true crimes. They are, by far, his favorite books. He has read hundreds of them and he knows what makes him turn pages and what bores him silly. He is the quintessential reader of true crimes, and so we will turn to him to see what at least one reader thinks.

As for what makes a good true crime, Allan has some definite preferences:

"To me a good true crime is about people doing things which, if you put it in a novel, nobody would believe it," he says. "Like the book *Beyond Belief* about people who were kidnapping children and making recordings of them. Also, these books are about people who can't see what's happening around them, and it seems inconceivable that they couldn't see it. Like in Jack Olsen's *Son*, it's so hard to believe that a woman can live with this man and not have a clue that he's going out and raping people every day.

"Also I like a book where the victim is chosen for a reason. I don't like books where the victims are picked at random and could be anybody. For example, I would not be interested in a book about the guy who did the shooting at the McDonald's. On the other hand, if it's about a postal worker who went back to work and murdered his fellow employees because he had a grudge against them, that would be okay. For me, there must be a reason for the victim to be the victim.

"There doesn't have to be a murder, and there doesn't have to be a lot of money. For me these books are a pyschological study. They are about the way people behave, and the good ones make you say, 'Aren't people amazing?' "

2
CHOOSING
THE STORY

WHERE TO LOOK

There is no crime shortage in North America. When was the last time you read a newspaper or listened to a local newscast without learning that someone had been garroted, knifed, shot, strangled, robbed, raped, embezzled, kidnapped or bilked out of a fortune?

Out of all those felonies in the news only a small percentage can be considered suspects for the true crime writer, but even that small percentage amounts to dozens of potential stories every week, and if you keep the news under constant surveillance you will eventually catch a good story.

The daily newspaper is the best place to seek stories that might be the germ of a true crime book. Read the local papers and once a week go to the library to read the out-of-town newspapers.

Also, let all of your friends know that you are hunting for a good true crime story. If they are at all decent, they will inform you about potential stories in their area. If there's a good story in New Jersey, for example, I'm going to know about it because my mother-in-law, Margie, sends me clippings from the *Newark Star-Ledger* every couple of months. Two years ago my brother Allan, who lives in Florida, sent me a small story from the *Miami Herald*, about a waitress at a pancake house who had been sent to death row, and reading that clipping became my first step toward writing *Without Mercy*. (It helps to have a brother who's a true crime aficionado. Also, note that I have written one Florida book and am writing another, but I have not yet written an Alaska book. When choosing a story, one must consider the climates where one will be spending a lot of time.)

You can also find potential stories in magazines. But keep in mind that if the writer sold the story to a magazine, maybe that was because the story wasn't strong enough to be a book. On the other hand, maybe the fellow who wrote the magazine article is polishing off the last ten pages of his fabulous book about the crime, while you're wondering whether or not you should look into it.

Still, check out anything that you think might be strong. I've seen dozens of articles in *People Weekly* that I thought had book potential, and many of them proved it by coming out between hard covers a year later.

Get some regional magazines like *Yankee* or *Texas Monthly*. At least a story published there hasn't been seen by every true crime writer in the country.

Watch the so-called "tabloid TV" shows. That is, watch them if they haven't gone the way of the Edsel. As I write this, tabloid TV shows like "Inside Edition" and "A Current Affair" are very big, but the phenomenon has the smell of a fad about it (Morton Downey, Jr. has already bitten the dust). Perhaps tabloid TV will become extinct in the near future, and you'll need to pick up a *real* tabloid (like the *National Enquirer*) at a supermarket checkout instead.

Watch talk shows like "The Oprah Winfrey Show," "The Phil Donahue Show" and "Geraldo." Sometimes the story you want is not the focus of the show. Oprah, for example, might do a show on "Victims of Rape," but maybe one of the guests happens to mention that the man who raped her was a psychiatrist who had written books on the psychology of the rapist. Maybe he could be the subject of your true crime book.

Also watch network magazine shows like "Sixty Minutes" and "20/20."

Talk to police, lawyers and prosecutors. There are good stories that never even get into the news, and those are the people who would know about them. Talk to reporters, too. They will remember stories in the news that, perhaps, snuck by you.

WHAT TO LOOK FOR

What follows is a list of elements you should look for in the initial news story. Not all true crime stories have all of these elements. This is not a scientific formula. But it is a fair generalization to say that your story must have at least two of these elements, and that if it doesn't, and you are not Joe McGinniss, Jack Olsen, Shana Alexander or Ann Rule, your story is deader than Jimmy Hoffa.

1. *An interesting criminal.* You're asking the reader to spend sev-

eral hundred pages with this person. It's not enough that he be cruel, devious, sadistic, psychotic and remorseless. Those are all fine qualities in a criminal. But is he fascinating? Is there something about him that made you pull the newspaper closer when you read it, or made you press the volume button on your TV remote control when you heard it? Jeffrey MacDonald in *Fatal Vision* was handsome and charming. William Douglas in *The Professor and the Prostitute* was an ordinary, somewhat shy, professor of biology. Adolfo Constanzo in my own book, *Across the Border*, was a charismatic homosexual who, allegedly, had psychic powers. What is it about your criminal that will make the reader sit up and take notice? Maybe the key is in his motivation. Maybe he only killed people who used the word "snuck," because it's not a real word and he is a fanatic about English.

And, by the way, throughout this book when I say "the criminal" I'm talking about the person or people in your book who are accused of the crime, even if they turn out to be innocent, as Anne Capute did in *Fatal Dosage*.

2. *An involved victim.* Sometimes victims in true crime books are people who were picked at random. But, as Allan suggests, those kinds of victims make for less interesting reading. Your story will have greater potential if the victims were chosen, like Jim and Naomi Olive who were killed by their daughter and her boyfriend in *Bad Blood: A Family Murder in Marin County*. A story is stronger if the victim somehow contributed, even in the most innocent ways, to his own death. (Of course, not all true crime victims are dead, but most of them are.)

3. *A sense of place.* Just as romance readers want to be transported to Paris or Rome or Hilton Head, the readers of true crime also seek that experience of visiting some place different. But for the true crime reader, the new location doesn't have to be glamorous or affluent or seventy degrees Fahrenheit year-round. It just has to be different.

Literary agent Russ Galen told me, "I think a sense of place is extremely important in true crimes. The reader wants to go some place exotic. Jack Olsen's book *Doc* takes place in Wyoming, where people still wear the ten-gallon hats and there are cowboys and ranchers. To people in Wyoming the book might be boring. But to everybody else that's exotic."

Lately, I've been reading *Appointment for Murder* by Susan Crain Bakos. The book takes place in St. Louis, in a "hardworking blue-collar community," it says on the back cover. Sounds pretty ordinary. But I live in a small farming community in New England, so for me this St. Louis neighborhood is exotic. Virtually any place can be made strange or exotic to most of your readers if you can identify the sense of place for yourself. In other words, which description of its "place" is most closely related to the crime or the criminal? Did the crime take place in "The Midwest" or did it really take place in "Kansas" or even perhaps "on the high wheat plains of western Kansas, a lonesome area that other Kansans call 'out there,' " as Truman Capote described his "place" in *In Cold Blood*?

4. *A different world.* "I think a true crime book should open up some world for the reader," says Charles Spicer at St. Martin's. "For example, we have a book called *Deadly Medicine*. In this case it's the world of medicine that is opened up for the reader. The book is about a nurse who was murdering children on a pediatric ward."

If you can find a clown who killed an acrobat, or a soap opera director who murdered his star, or even a Detroit auto worker who murdered several co-workers and stuffed their bodies into the gas tanks of new cars, you might have something. Like the "sense of place" the "world" doesn't have to be glamorous. The important thing is that it be relevant. If the auto worker killed his first two wives, but the murders were totally unrelated to assembly lines, union politics, the pressure to produce cars, or the killer's hatred of Japanese imports you're probably not going to be able to transport the reader into a different world.

5. *Complications.* These are a little more difficult to pin down, and often the initial news story doesn't reveal them. When I hear about a crime I wait for the sound of the other shoe dropping. That's what I call complications. It's not enough to have a woman kill her co-worker, even if she does it in a bizarre way and buries the body in an odd place. There has to be more. Graves can be shallow, but stories cannot. There must be a twist, not necessarily a shocking twist such as you find in a mystery novel, but the kind of twist where you tell somebody what happened and they find it interesting and then you say, "and that's not all," or "wait 'til you hear the rest of it."

Taking my own book, *Without Mercy*, for example, if my killers had simply murdered Art Venecia and buried his body in his own yard, then confessed a year later, it would have been interesting, but not bookworthy. But that's not what happened. They murdered Art Venecia and buried him in the yard, *and then* Art's mother started asking too many questions, so they murdered her, too, *and then* they took over Art's identity and sold off his yacht, and his stocks and bonds and his house.

If your story has no *and then*s chances are it won't work.

One more point before we go on. I often get calls from people who want to write a true crime book about a case, and I ask "What's the case?"

"Well, my husband's nephew has been arrested for robbing several liquor stores."

"What's the story?"

"Well, he was an abused kid. My husband's brother is a drinker. And the mother, Lillian, well she's always been a troubled person. I'm not surprised that Larry's in trouble. He's a basically good kid, and I think the book could help with his legal expenses."

Don't make the mistake of thinking a book should be written about a crime, just because you happen to have some personal connection to it. The person who pays $19.95 for a book couldn't care less about whether the subject is the author's nephew. He wants an interesting book. Even if your cousin Lydia strangles her housekeeper with a toaster cord, the story isn't any stronger just because she's your cousin. Make sure you are choosing stories because they are fascinating to readers, not because they are convenient for you.

A CASE HISTORY

Okay, so you've found a true crime story in the *Sacramento Bee*, or on "The Phil Donahue Show," and you're certain you could write a publishable book about it. What's next? You have to do some preliminary exploration before you get in too deep. You need to talk to people. Who do you talk to and what do you ask? Well, let's take a real case history.

The first time I heard of the Florida pancake house murders was when I read the *Miami Herald* news clipping, which my brother sent me.

WAITRESS GETS DEATH PENALTY

First woman in Dade to be sentenced to die. By Jay Ducassi, Herald staff writer.

Dee Dyne Casteel, a Naranja waitress who paid two car mechanics to commit murder, was sentenced to the electric chair Wednesday, the first time a woman has been sentenced to death in a Dade court.

Circuit Judge Ralph Person sentenced Casteel, 49, to death for the 1983 murder of Bessie Fischer. The victim, 84 years old, had begun asking for her missing son, whom Casteel and a fellow employee had ordered killed a month before.

A 12-member jury unanimously recommended the death penalty for Casteel after convicting her of both murders in July.

"Casteel contacted the murderers, delivered the money, arranged for the murderers to get into the trailer of Bessie Fischer, introduced the murderers to Ms. Fischer, then walked away knowing they were going to murder her," the judge said, reading from a ten-page sentencing order.

Person also sentenced James Allen Bryant, 29, the man who planned the murders with Casteel, to death. The sentences came a day after Person sent the two contract killers, Michael Irvine and William Rhodes to death row.

The story drew me, but I was still miles away from being sure that I wanted to write a book about it. I had to know more.

When you first meet a story, whether it is through a news clipping or a television show that you taped on your VCR, look for names. They are your sources of additional information. In this story there were the names of the four killers, but I knew I couldn't get in touch with any of them quickly. There was also the name of the judge, but I suspected that he would be reluctant to talk about the case. I would have called him if I had to. But there was another name that could direct me to more sources. The reporter, Jay Ducassi. For every story, there is a reporter. Find out where he got his information.

I called Ducassi at the *Miami Herald* and he told me that Dee Casteel had a daughter, Susan, who worked at some correctional facility in Dade county. I called the various Dade county prisons until I found her. From Susan, I was able to get the names of Dee's lawyer, her friends, and people who worked at the pancake house. When I started calling Dee's friends, they told me, in various ways, "Dee Casteel is the nicest person you could ever want to meet, she's a real sweetheart."

I was hooked. The nicest person I could ever want to meet was on death row for two murders. I knew I had a story.

But knowing that a story could be a good book, and deciding to write it, are two different things. There are a number of things you want to find out first.

Will You Get Cooperation?

Probably your story can be written without the cooperation of any one or two people, but if nobody of significance will cooperate with you, you've got serious problems. Of course, the people whose cooperation you need varies with each story, but here is a list that applies to most true crime ideas.

1. *The criminal, or criminals.* Try to gauge how honest he will be with you, how much time you will get with him, and how you can verify his information elsewhere.

2. *The criminal's lawyer.* When you are writing a true crime book, a lawyer can be your best friend or your worst enemy. Lawyers can open doors for you, get you files, depositions, transcripts. But they can also slam doors shut. If a lawyer advises his client not to speak to you, chances are the client will be as silent as a giraffe. Try to convince the lawyer that the book is in the client's best interest, and that it will also make the lawyer look good. Lawyers, despite reports to the contrary, are human beings. They respond to stroking. A subtle reminder that such books often get made into movies will help, and if you can unobtrusively slip the phrase "celebrity lawyer" into the conversation it can do wonders.

3. *Friends and relatives of the criminal.* If the criminal will not cooperate with you, chances are he will write to his friends and tell them to be equally unreceptive.

4. *People who knew the criminal, fellow employees, etc.* This is rarely a problem. If enough people knew the criminal, you'll find people who will be delighted to talk about him. (With these people, as with the lawyer, and everybody else, it might help to mention the possibility of the book being made into a movie. People are merely impressed by book writers, but they are thoroughly dazzled by moviemakers.)

5. *The criminal's jailor.* If the criminal is in jail you need to know how much access you will have to him. Call the warden or prison superintendent and find out how much visiting time you will be allowed.

6. *The victim or victims.* If the victim refuses to talk to you, and there's no other way to get his information, you might consider looking for another story.

7. *The victim's close friends and relatives.* These people will probably go along with whatever the victim decides. If the victim is

dead, chances are you will find friends or relatives who are willing to talk about him.

8. *People who knew the victim.* Again, this is not a problem. Unless the victim was Grizzly Adams or someone equally hermitic, he had a lot of acquaintances, and some of them will talk to you.

9. *The prosecutor on the case.* If the prosecutor thinks you are going to write a "miscarriage of justice" story, he will not be anxious to help you. Also, he might be prevented from talking to you by law or administrative directive. On the other hand, he's probably proud of the work he did on the case, and anxious to talk about it. If he is politically ambitious, he will see at a glance the publicity benefits of being portrayed in your book as the crusader for truth, justice and the American way.

10. *The investigating police officers.* Police are usually as cooperative as their superiors allow them to be. A lot depends on whether they think the book will make them look good or bad.

You should call these people, tell them you are planning to write a book, and ask if they will be willing to grant interviews. If most of them say no, take the hint. Move on to another story.

There are many reasons why people might be unwilling to cooperate with you. If a lawyer thinks publicity could hurt his client's appeal, then he will advise the client not to talk to you. If the case is highly publicized you'll find, as I did with *Across the Border*, that some of the people involved are trying to make book or movie deals of their own. Sometimes people just don't want their situations made any more public than they already are. Sometimes people are afraid. When I wrote *Across the Border*, some people wouldn't talk to me because they thought Adolfo Constanzo, the cult leader, would rise from the grave and punish them.

How Much Will It Cost to Write the Story?

Many true crime writers stake out a territory and only look for stories in that area. Ann Rule, for example, writes about crimes in the northwest United States. Obviously, a writer will know his own area best, and choosing stories in that area will allow him to sleep in his own bed at night. But another reason for sticking close to home is money. Travel is expensive.

If your story is far away from your home, how many days will you have to spend out of town? How much is the air fare? How expensive are motels in the area? What about restaurants?

The reality is that if you live in Rhode Island and the story is in Hawaii and you're not an established true crime writer who can get big advances, it is extremely unlikely that you can write the book profitably.

But if you are drawn to stories out of town, you need to estimate your travel time. Of course there is no perfect formula for figuring the amount of travel time you will need, but I can give you a few guidelines. If you are going to read and take notes on an entire court file and depositions, and you're going to do it in the courthouse to save the expense of photocopying records, you should allow yourself four full days.

There will be a number of people that you will want to interview in person. Some people won't do phone interviews. Some, you'll just want to meet in person so you can see how they carry themselves. And some are in jail where they don't have access to a phone. Assuming everything goes smoothly and people are available when you want them, you still should plan one day in town for every three people you want to interview.

Also you'll need two or three days just to visit the locations associated with the case, and to take notes for that "sense of place" material that is so important to your book.

Also allow at least one full day for reading newspaper stories at the local library.

In addition to travel expenses, there are long-distance phone calls to consider, and the cost of photos which you will have to supply with the book, and if you are going to need a trial transcript that's going to cost a bundle.

Of course, the significance of your expense figure depends on the book's potential to make money, which can't be gauged at this point. So I can't give you a formula like: Go ahead if the expenses will be under $4,000. All I'm saying is try to estimate the expenses and put that information in the pot with all the rest before you move on to the next step.

WILL YOU HAVE TO SHARE MONEY?

Often the criminal or the victim will only tell you his story if you will divvy up with him the money that you get for the book. The arrangement can be anything you agree on, but fifty-fifty is most common. Sometimes it's worth it, sometimes it's not. With *Fatal Dosage* and *Finder* I shared the money in return for full and exclusive cooperation. With *Without Mercy* and *Across the Border* I did not.

In the case of *Without Mercy* I could not have shared money even if I'd wanted to. Florida has a so-called "Son of Sam" law, which makes it illegal for a criminal to earn money from his crimes by selling book or movie rights. To find out if a state has a "Son of Sam" law, call the state Attorney General's office in the state capital.

With *Fatal Dosage*, I went fifty-fifty with Anne Capute, and that was the wise thing to do. In return I had exclusive access to Anne's family, as well as her lawyer and his files, including interviews, depositions, and a trial transcript that would have cost me thousands. Without that cooperation it would have been virtually impossible to write the book. On the other hand, with *Across the Border* I didn't share money because no one person's piece of the information pie was big enough, or exclusive enough.

Keep in mind that sharing money often means sharing credit too, and more often than not the writer is the person who gets the least of it. Many true crime books have two "authors" but only one writer. *Perfect Victim*, for example, is the joint effort of Christine McGuire, the prosecutor on the case, and Carla Norton, the writer. If you write a book in the first person of someone else's viewpoint, as I did with *Finder*, you will get second billing or none at all. (I got second billing and smaller print.) None of this, of course, is reason enough to jettison a project. But it's one more thing to think about.

Do You Have to Get Approval to Publish?

Even though I split the money with Anne Capute I made it clear from the beginning, and Anne agreed, that only I would decide what would go into the book and what would not. In that respect, Anne was a writer's dream come true. She gave me a free hand and never asked me to change a word, even though there must have been passages that made her cringe.

As far as I'm concerned this is not a negotiable issue. I must have absolute control over what I write. As soon as the subject of a book gets the power of approval, all credibility is lost. The reader looks to the writer as an unbiased expert on the case, and wants to know what the writer thinks. A book about a woman who was allegedly framed for murder is not very compelling if we get the feeling that she's the only one who is saying she was framed. Furthermore, handing over the power of approval is risky. What if you finish your book, and then the subject decides he doesn't like it? You've just wasted a year or more of your professional life.

IS ANYBODY ELSE WRITING ABOUT THE CASE?

There have been cases that have inspired more than one successful book. *Nutcracker* by Shana Alexander and *At Mother's Request* by Jonathan Coleman, for example, were about the same case. There are three books about the so-called "Mormon Murders." In several cases there have been instant paperbacks rushed out to bookstores while a case is fresh in the public mind, followed a year or more later by more substantial hardcover books. (*Across the Border* is an example. As I write this there are at least four more books being written on the same subject.)

But realistically, if you discover that somebody is already writing a book on the case you're interested in you should probably back off unless it's an extraordinary story that can sustain more than one book. Before you retreat, however, investigate to find out just who it is that's writing the book and whether or not he has a publishing contract. Often you will hear that someone is writing a book, and it will be only a rumor. Other times the alleged writer turns out to be some relative or friend who possesses no writing skills and has less chance of getting a book published than he does of becoming governor of Oklahoma.

WILL YOU HAVE TO CHECK UNDER THE BED EVERY NIGHT?

Will a rock be thrown through your window? Will your tires be slashed? Will you be slashed? When I was writing *Without Mercy* I endured occasional moments of concern that one of my murderer-subjects would file his way through the bars of death row and hitchhike north to pay a nocturnal visit to "that writer." When I began *Across the Border* I sometimes worried that satanic cultists would lay in wait for me behind the oil burner in my cellar. Such thoughts are normal even if they are irrational. (Is the killer who has been fingered by a cohort, arrested by police, disappointed by a lawyer, excoriated by a prosecutor, sentenced by a judge, imprisoned by guards, and mistreated by fellow prisoners, really going to put a book writer at the top of his hit list?) I'm sure that all true crime writers have occasional fits of paranoia. After all, we're dealing with some pretty despicable lowlifes, and they sometimes have despicable friends and relatives.

But fret not. Being a true crime writer isn't really hazardous to your health. I don't know of any writer who has ever had his typewriter sealed in concrete, tied around his neck, and dumped in the East River. But the possibility of danger is one more thing you want to consider before you decide to write a book. Is your book likely to threaten anyone who is unstable or prone to violence? Are you going to discover and reveal who really killed those three slow pizza parlor workers? Are you going to make public the guilt of someone who so far has gone unpunished? Think about it.

The question is not just: Are you in danger? The question is: Are you going to worry about the fact that you might be in danger? If you spend all your writing time looking over your shoulder and jumping every time a twig falls off a tree outside your writing room, you're not going to enjoy writing the story, so you should pass on it.

IS THE STORY COMPLETE?

"For the better part of two years Truman's life was in a state of suspended animation," Gerald Clarke writes in *Capote*. "He could not finish his book until he had an ending, but neither could he put it aside and go on to something else."

The book, of course, is *In Cold Blood*, and what happened to Capote could happen to you. He needed to know the fate of his killers, Hickock and Smith, before he could finish his book, but their death sentences were under appeal, a process which lasts longer than most marriages.

That is not to say that you should reject a good story idea just because the criminal's sentence is under appeal. It depends on how you see the story. Dee Casteel, for example, appealed her sentence, but that didn't affect my writing plans, because to me her story ends when she is sentenced. On the other hand, if I had started writing my book when news of her arrest hit the newspapers I would have been sorry, because it took three years for the case to come to trial.

So you need to decide if all the events that make your idea a good story have already occurred, and if they haven't, how long they are likely to take. Keep in mind that the publishers are going to have the same concern, and you may not be able to get a publishing contract if the ending of your book is uncertain, or if there's no telling when the case will end.

EIGHT STORIES I REJECTED AND WHY

Just as you don't marry the first girl you date, you don't usually write the first true crime story that you investigate. The professional true crime writer knows that he's going to be spending a year or two with his story, so he chooses carefully. He thinks about many stories and dismisses most of them quickly from his mind. With others, he makes a few phone calls and writes a few letters. He tries to get the information that we have discussed here. And then, for one reason or another he discards them. Here are eight ideas that I have thought about and then rejected in the past year.

1. *The Gentleman Bandit.* This was a young man down in South Carolina who was robbing banks. He was good looking and charming. When he robbed banks he wore a three-piece suit and he was always extremely courteous to his victims and their customers. Furthermore, he was the son of a general and a former real estate agent on swank Hilton Head Island.

The story appealed to me because of the sense of place, affluent Hilton Head. And of course the whole idea of a well-to-do, educated young man robbing banks made for an interesting character. The only reason I didn't pursue the story was that I didn't think bank robbery was a strong enough crime to sustain fascination for the character. If he had murdered people, even accidentally during a holdup, I probably would have gotten on the phone to examine the story more closely.

2. *The Little Old Southern Lady and the Arsenic.* If you think you've read this story, that's the problem. I'm thinking about a woman in North Carolina who has been accused of killing several of the men in her life with arsenic. It is appealing because she is "the nice little old lady whom no one would suspect" and because of the enormity of her alleged crimes.

But on the downside there is the fact that the story, if it turns out to be true, sounds familiar. There have been many cases of little old ladies in the South spicing the food of their menfolk with arsenic, and some of the cases have been published as true crime books.

3. *The Chicken Soup Murder.* This is a story about a guy in New York who, allegedly, murdered his girlfriend, cut up her body, then

boiled the flesh off her bones and carried them around the city in a bucket.

I was drawn to the story because it was bizarre, because an editor encouraged me to look into it, and because it looked like an opportunity to explore the world of the homeless street people in lower Manhattan. But when I looked into the case, it seemed that the alleged murderer was such a raving psycho-wacko that even total cooperation from him would be almost worthless.

4. *The Missing Girl in Arkansas.* Some Arkansas neighbors of the missing girl's family asked me to write about it. The mother first claimed to have killed her daughter, then changed her story to say that her daughter had disappeared. Then she changed it again to say that a boyfriend had killed the daughter. Later, she decided that a school bus driver had taken her daughter.

I was attracted to the world of the small town in Arkansas, where almost every citizen was looking for the girl. But I rejected the story because the girl had not been found, and until she was, there would be no way to verify or refute any of the mother's stories.

5. *The Man Who Killed His Family and Lived Another Life for Seventeen Years.* This, the case of John List, is a New Jersey story that got gallons of publicity in the New York–New Jersey area, where many writers and almost everybody in publishing, lives. I knew that dozens of writers would jump on it. Indeed, one editor later told me, "Every editor in New York has twenty List proposals on her desk." It was a good story, but not worth competing with all those other writers for.

6. *The Stuart Case.* This case is easily the most publicized of the past several years, and it occurred in my own backyard, Boston. Charles Stuart reported that he had been wounded and his pregnant wife shot to death by a black assailant one night when they were returning from a childbirth class at a local hospital. Though at that point it seemed to be just "one more shooting in the city," it had a galvanizing effect on Boston and became the symbol for street crime that had gotten out of hand. Politicians, police and newspeople could talk of little else. Even then, long before there was any indication that there was more to the story, I thought of writing a book about the case. However, I realized it was not really a true crime story; it would be a book about a city finally blowing its stack over crime in the streets. Best leave it to a sociologist to write, I decided.

Several weeks after the crime, Charles Stuart jumped off a bridge and it became clear that there had been no black assailant. Stuart had murdered his own wife. The story was a sensation, a potentially great true crime story, and everybody I knew called to ask if I was going to write the book, since I live near Boston. I would have loved to have done the book, but I was already committed to another book and this story was so hot that it was impossible to wait and do it later. Certainly books and movies were being created almost immediately. As it turned out the first book on the case, *Murder in Boston* was written by Ken Englade, whose comments appear elsewhere in this book.

7. *The Ex-Playboy Bunny Who Might Have Been Framed by the Police.* When I first heard about Milwaukee's Lawrencia Bembenek, a thirty-one-year-old beauty who had been a Playboy bunny and a police officer, I knew I had the makings of a successful true crime book and movie. Bembenek had been tried and convicted of killing her husband's ex-wife, but there was a strong possibility that she was innocent and had been set up because of earlier criticism of the police.

I wrote to Lawrencia and she wrote back saying she would be glad to work with me, but warning me that there was another true crime writer working on the case. Unfortunately the other writer was a very big name in the business, Vincent Bugliosi of *Helter Skelter* fame, so I backed away.

As it happens, several months later Lawrencia escaped from prison with a man she was engaged to marry. Her story became very big news and the public sided with her. In Milwaukee sympathizers wore sweatshirts that said, "Run Bambi Run!" She has become a bit of a legend.

So my decision to stay away from the story was either a mistake, because it is now bigger than ever, or brilliant because she may never be caught.

8. *The Nice Boys Who Raped the Retarded Girl.* This is a story that's been going on in New Jersey in some nice affluent community. The gist of the thing is that these were nice kids who did an unspeakable act and ruined their lives and damaged the lives of those around them. The town, apparently, is in shock.

My reason for rejecting this story, which is getting a lot of publicity, is perhaps the best reason of all—I am not strongly drawn to it.

You have to have a feeling for a story, a sense that "this is right for me." I don't have that here. Perhaps another writer will come along and write a fabulous book about this case, or any of these that I rejected. That doesn't mean I was wrong about the case. It just means I wasn't the best writer for the story.

So there are eight story ideas rejected for eight different reasons. You will have your own ideas, your own rejections, your own reasons. But sooner or later you will hit upon the story that you want, the one that has characters that fascinate you, and events that excite you. You'll find yourself writing it in your head, thinking of angles, imagining scenes, planning your research, trying on titles. You'll even be able to envision the finished book in your head. When that happens you'll know that this is the story for you, and that you are the best writer for the story.

3
THE PROPOSAL

SCREEN THE IDEA

If you have a literary agent you should screen the story idea with her first. The agent, if she has handled many true crimes, will tell you that it's a great idea or a lousy idea, and she will tell you why she thinks so.

If you've established a relationship with an editor at a publishing house, and he is the person to whom you want to sell your true crime book, then you should screen the idea with him, also.

Neither of these people is the last word on the merits of your project. But they are in the business, and you should listen to, and consider, what they have to say.

However, since you are reading this book, chances are you have never sold a true crime book before. Perhaps you are a pre-published writer. In any case, I am going to assume that you have no agent and no editor who is calling you up and begging you to write a true crime.

WHAT IS A PROPOSAL?

When I write a nonfiction book I never write it first and then sell it. I always sell it first and then write it. That's how professional nonfiction writers work. Nobody wants to spend a year on a true crime book and then find out that there are no buyers.

The way to sell a book in advance is by submitting a proposal. The proposal, simply, is an attempt to convince a publisher that you can write a good book that can be published profitably. If the publisher likes your proposal, you will receive a contract to write the book.

The proposal is made up of three main parts.

1. A letter
2. An outline
3. Sample chapters

THE LETTER

The letter should be addressed to the editor you want to reach. Never send a proposal just to a publishing house. Always send it to a name. How do you get the name you want? We'll discuss that later.

Your letter is the editor's introduction to you and, probably, to the case. It should tell the editor what happened, who it happened to, and what the result was. It should indicate those "layers," that Charles Spicer spoke of, that is, it should strongly imply that this book will have depth, characters, surprises. You should tell the editor why you think this story should be a book, how you plan to approach the project, and how much cooperation you expect to get. Your letter should communicate your enthusiasm about the project; it should make him curious. The letter should have the same effect as the back cover of a paperback true crime. It should make the reader want to buy the book or, at least, turn to page one and start reading.

I'm going to give you some examples of real letters that were included with proposals for my books. But before I do that, I have to digress a bit and talk about titles, for reasons that will become clear soon.

A Digression About Titles. When it comes to titles, publishers always think that they are smarter than writers. Specifically, marketing directors at publishing houses fancy themselves title experts, and so it is quite common for a true crime book to be written and contracted for under one title, which is then tossed into the wastebasket, and published under another title.

When I wrote the book which is known as *Fatal Dosage*, I called it *Anne's Story*. When I wrote *Without Mercy*, it was *Delirium*. And when I wrote *Across the Border* I called it *Crossing the Line*.

I don't know whether this is good or bad. Maybe marketing people do know which titles will sell the most books; after all, that's their business. In any case this business of having your title changed is a reality, and you should know about it. I'm telling you about it now because the letters that follow are the originals and they refer to the books by the title I had in mind at the time. So keep in mind that *Anne's Story* means *Fatal Dosage* and *Delirium* means *Without Mercy*.

EXAMPLES OF LETTERS

I'm going to show you the letter I wrote in the *Delirium* proposal, because I'll later use the outline from the same proposal. But if I included only that letter you would say, "Well, that's great Gary, I'm happy for you that you sold the book. But, unlike me, you already had two true crime books behind you, don't you think that helped?"

Of course, it helped. That's why I'm also including the letter for *Fatal Dosage*, my first true crime book.

Shirley Fogelberg
Senior Editor
Bantam Books
666 Fifth Avenue
New York, New York 10103

Dear Shirley Fogelberg:

Like most people in New England, and millions of others across the country, I was aware of the "Capute Case" as it unfolded in the press and under the eye of the television camera. Anne Capute and two other nurses at Morton Hospital in Taunton, Massachusetts, had been accused of a mercy killing. They were charged with murdering terminally ill Norma C. Leanues, by deliberately injecting her with 195 milligrams of morphine. As the case progressed, the public spotlight narrowed to focus only on Anne Capute, age forty-four, mother of seven, who was tried and acquitted for first-degree murder in Fall River, Massachusetts.

But it wasn't until after the trial, when I met Anne and was asked to prepare a book proposal about the Capute case, that I realized what a great story this is. The Anne Capute story has all the twists and crises and characters of the most successful fiction. But Anne's Story is true.

I propose to write Anne's Story, the story of the Anne Capute murder trial.

It is a story about a middle-aged woman who had always wanted to be a nurse, who entered nursing school at the age of forty while still raising three of her four daughters.

It is the story of an ordinary woman from Plympton, Massachusetts, who was suddenly thrust before the public eyes, and discussed in every bar and diner in the state.

It is the story of a woman who lost her job, her profession, her anonymity, her marriage, and a dear friend, who went thousands of dollars into debt, and yet says today that she would not erase the past, "because I learned so much, I grew so much."

Enclosed are my sample chapters and outline for Anne's Story. I hope you find this tale as compelling as I do.

Sincerely,

Gary Provost

Jeanette Stone
Senior Editor
Pocket Books
Simon and Schuster Building
1230 Avenue of the Americas
New York, New York 10020

Dear Jeanette Stone:

I propose to write <u>Delirium: A True Story of Murder Under the Influence,</u> the story about Dee Casteel, an "ordinary woman" who is now on death row in Florida for her part in two bizarre murders. Dee is the first woman to be sentenced to the electric chair from Dade county, which includes Miami and Miami Beach.

Dee Casteel was a waitress at an International House of Pancakes. She and the restaurant manager, Allen Bryant, hired Michael Irvine and William Rhodes to murder Arthur Venecia, owner of the restaurant. Venecia had been Bryant's homosexual lover for eight years. Irvine and Rhodes were two more "ordinary people." Not professional criminals, they were mechanics at a nearby Amoco station.

After Venecia's throat was slit Dee and Bryant hid the body in Venecia's garage. Later they buried him in his own front yard. They took over Venecia's house, his yacht, his stocks and the pancake house. They told friends and employees that Venecia had gone away. They sold off Venecia's assets to pay for some high living. For some transactions Bryant assumed Venecia's identity.

In time Bessie Fischer, Venecia's mother, started asking questions, so they strangled her with a nylon stocking and they buried her with her son. Almost a year went by before the crimes were discovered. Later, Dade county police described it as "almost the perfect crime." But it all fell apart because the criminals turned against each other. They were caught. Dee, Bryant, Irvine and Rhodes were all tried this past summer, and all have been sentenced to die in the electric chair.

The thing that fascinates me about this case is that everybody who knows Dee describes her as a sweet, nice, helpful lady. I intend to write a book about how she got from being a nice person to being a person who hires killers. The explanation, to a large extent, is alcohol, and a weakness for men who treated her poorly. She was a woman who drank too much and loved too much.

I am the only author who has interviewed the main characters in this case and read the court file. I can confidently say that no other books on this case are being written. Already I have movie interest in the project. I will need a year to complete the book.

I am the author of <u>Fatal Dosage</u>, the true story of Anne Capute, a nurse who was accused of a mercy killing and tried for first-degree murder. The

31

book was a Bantam lead title and has been sold to CBS for a television movie.

I also wrote <u>Finder</u>, the story of Marilyn Greene, the nation's leading finder of missing people. The book, which will be published by Crown this spring, already has a $50,000 paperback floor and has been optioned for film by Warner Brothers for $50,000.

Thanks for reading. If you have any questions, please give me a call.

Sincerely,

Gary Provost

Your Credits. Your writing credits should appear someplace in the proposal, usually in the letter, as some of mine do in the *Delirium* letter. I have a "credit sheet," a form which has all my credits on it, and I usually include that with my proposal. That's fine if you have published a lot of material. But if you've only got a few publishing credits, they're going to look awfully lonely on that sheet of paper, so it is better to include them in the letter. Something like, "My article on the Gregory Richard kidnapping appeared in *Rolling Stone*, in May, and I have also published nonfiction in *TV Guide*, the *New York Times*, and a dozen local and regional publications."

If you have not published a book or any articles in major magazines, it's going to be difficult to sell your book, but not impossible. Many true crime books have been written by local reporters who have never freelanced, but did cover the case they are writing about. Also, keep in mind, whether you've published no books or a hundred books, your goal is the same: You are trying to convince an editor that you can write this true crime book and that people will buy it.

THE OUTLINE

As you proceed through your writing career your outlines shrink. Editors get to know you. They learn that you can deliver. They trust your judgment. Jack Olsen says, "My outline consists of four sentences over the phone to my agent," and, "If I did write an outline I wouldn't make it more than three pages because they wouldn't read it."

Well that's fine if you're the author of best-sellers like *Son* and

Cold Kill. On the other hand, I know writers who submit eighty-page outlines.

I can assure you that if you are writing your first true crime proposal, you are not going to sell it with a four-sentence outline. However, you don't have to write eighty pages, either. Something between ten and twenty pages should be just fine.

The outline, incidentally, is not etched in marble. It describes the book as you see it at this early stage. Editors understand that new information will be revealed to you in the research, new characters will appear, the story will twist in ways that you hadn't known about at the time of the proposal. If you get a contract for your book and then discover that the story you are writing is slightly different from the one you proposed, you don't have to put in a frantic call to your editor. However, if you seem to be headed down a very different path, if the cold-hearted murderer you proposed to write about turns out to be a fine citizen who was framed, it might be a good idea to give your editor a call and talk about how the book is going to be written.

Here is the outline I submitted with my *Delirium* proposal.

DELIRIUM
A True Story of Murder Under the Influence
By Gary Provost

OUTLINE

Chapter One: THE SCHEME
Bryant calls Dee and asks her to meet him. They go for a drive. Bryant hints that he would like to kill Art Venecia. He asks Dee if she knows someone who will murder for money. Dee says her friend, Mike Irvine, might know somebody.

Chapter Two: THE WOMAN
Dee goes to Mike Irvine, asks if he knows somebody who would kill for money. Irvine says he might do it himself if the price is right. Dee begins to act as go-between for Bryant and Irvine.

Who is this woman, acting as go-between for a hired murder? Here I will go into Dee's background. She was abandoned by her parents at an early age, grew up with her grandmother. At eighteen Dee turns to alcohol. At twenty-one her husband is gone and she has three kids. Though she is drinking, her life seems to be under control. She is very bright and has good jobs, first as an assistant to the mayor, later as an executive secretary in a large firm. But with no husband and three kids, she is desperate for money. She embezzles ten thousand dollars from the company, and she is caught. She does not go to jail, but her settlement with the company prevents her from ever taking another responsible position. She becomes a waitress, and she never commits another crime until the Venecia murder. There are many men in the following years, and all of them treat her poorly. What makes her drink? What draws her to the wrong kind of men?

Against all this we also see Dee as the kind, loving person. She is a good mother and a good friend. People who know her think the world of her.

Chapter Three: THE LOVERS

After Bryant makes plans with Irvine he changes his mind. He doesn't want to pay the twenty-five hundred dollars which they have agreed to. He and Dee drive to Key West to buy a gun, in Dee's name. They can kill Venecia themselves, he tells her, then they'll be on easy street: the house, the money, the restaurant, etc.

Here I will give the reader the background on James Allen Bryant and Arthur Venecia. Bryant is the spoiled, troubled boy who is desperately afraid that his mother will find out he is homosexual. Venecia, the successful, likable businessman who is openly, but not obviously, gay. Venecia is a lover of culture, of flowers, a patron of the arts. The relationship is stormy. Bryant often steals from Venecia, but Venecia always takes him back. Unknown to Venecia, Bryant has other boyfriends. With one, Felix, he engages in bizarre rituals, such as killing a chicken and drinking its blood. What needs are Bryant and Venecia fulfilling for each other?

Bryant and Dee go to Venecia's house with the gun. Bryant goes in to see if he can set up a situation for a killing. Dee, soused and frightened, stays outside, sits on a stool, and puts her head on the window air conditioner. She falls asleep. Nothing happens.

Chapter Four: THE KILLERS

Bryant and Irvine finally agree on a time, a place and a price for the murder. Irvine, afraid to do it alone, enlists William "Joker" Rhodes, who works at the gas station with him.

Who are these men who are willing to murder for money? Here I will go into the background of Irvine and Rhodes. Irvine is the gentle, likable man who, friends say, goes on a drinking binge about once a year and gets nasty. Irvine has been selling dope lately, but has no criminal record. Rhodes is the drifter with a criminal record, from Springfield, Illinois.

Chapter Five: THE FIRST MURDER

(At this point the book will funnel more narrowly into Dee's point of view. I think it will be stronger that way because of the way in which I can reveal information and, more importantly, because it will give the reader the Dee character to identify with during this tense, dramatic period.)

Dee begins to realize that this murder plan is real. Art is really going to be killed. She is a confusion of feelings. She is proud that Bryant has depended on her. She is excited about the money and the responsible position she will have in the restaurant. She is frightened by the idea of the murders, and afraid that she might be murdered if she tells police. She is anxious to have it over with. She begins to make phone calls to her daughter Susan, who is now living in Fort Lauderdale. At first she hints, "Bryant and I are working on a plan." Later she tells Susan, "We're going to murder Art."

Now Susan is confused. Should she tell the police? She can't, this is her own mother. Is it even real? Probably not, just her mother's drunken ramblings. Susan tells herself the murder is never going to happen.

The night of the murder Bryant, Irvine and Rhodes meet at the pancake house. They drive to Art Venecia's house. They come back at midnight. Irvine and Rhodes leave. Bryant tells Dee that they have done it. They have murdered Art.

Chapter Six: THE STORY

Dee and Bryant return to Venecia's house the next morning. They clean up the blood and drag the body into the garage attached to the house.

Venecia's mother, Bessie Fischer, in her eighties and close to senility, lives in a trailer on the five-acre Venecia property. Dee goes to her and tells her that Art has gone away for a while on business. Dee makes lunch for Bessie, starts to take care of the old lady, bringing her meals every day.

Bryant and Dee go to the pancake house. Bryant calls all the employees together and announces that Art Venecia has gone away for a long time to South Carolina to pursue other things. Bryant will be the boss now, but he won't be around much. Dee Casteel will be the manager of the restaurant. The employees accept this, though after several weeks rumors begin to arise that Venecia is dead.

Dee has called Susan and told her about the murder. Susan freaks out; has an emotional breakdown. She can't live with what she knows, and she can't turn her mother in. She starts to drink to drown her knowledge. Susan begins a steady slide downward, which will eventually include drugs, and some prostitution.

Dee, despite being tortured by her knowledge and heavy drinking, remains in control. She runs the restaurant, she tells the fake story. It seems they have gotten away with it.

Chapter Seven: THE SECOND MURDER

A month has gone by. People are curious about Art's disappearance but nobody is alarmed. He had no close friends or relatives except his mother. His mother is asking questions every day. The killers had hoped she would die of natural causes. Now they are getting edgy. Bryant tells Dee that Bessie will have to be killed. Dee objects. Bryant talks her into it. Dee brings Irvine and Rhodes to the trailer, telling Bessie they are there to fix the roof. Dee leaves. Irvine and Rhodes choke Bessie to death with a nylon stocking.

Chapter Eight: THE HOUSE

Dee moves out of her rented house and into Venecia's house with Todd, Wayne and Susan. The boys ask no questions; they have moved many times in the past. Susan, of course, knows about the murders. Dee hires Susan to work at the pancake house. She needs her daughter, her closest friend, near her. Dee shows Susan the bodies.

By this time the bodies have been moved to a tin barn at the front of the property, but they are beginning to stink. Dee and Bryant decide they must be buried. Dee calls a backhoe operator to dig a huge hole in the front yard. She and Bryant bury the bodies.

Sometimes Bryant comes by with his Cuban boyfriends, picks up Dee, and they go drinking, but Bryant never actually enters the house where the murder took place. He sometimes leaves cocaine for Susan who is now using the drug. Sometimes they all go to the dog track together and Bryant makes thousand dollar bets. He is drawing large amounts of money out of the restaurant, shortchanging the national IHOP franchise operation, not paying bills. This is a reckless, wild time that requires more and more money.

Chapter Nine: THE SELLING

Bryant assumes the identity of Arthur Venecia in order to sell off

Venecia's property. With Dee acting as agent, they sell Art's two old cars; then his camper; then the trailer that Bessie lived in; then the yacht; stocks and bonds; an expensive organ; and finally, the house itself. Incredibly, they manage to sell the house without getting caught, even though they ask for payment in cash, and Bryant cannot produce any identification to prove he's Venecia.

Chapter Ten: THE FALLING OUT

The four conspirators begin bickering. Dee is angry at Irvine and Rhodes because they didn't "finish the job they were hired for." They didn't dispose of the body. Bryant and Dee are angry with Irvine because he stole jewelry out of Bessie's trailer and didn't split with them. Rhodes finds out that Irvine shortchanged him on the payment for the murder. Rhodes vows to find Irvine and kill him. Dee is angry with Bryant. He has been selling all these expensive items and instead of giving her half the money he is giving her a hundred bucks here and there. She has bought a small house for a fifteen hundred dollar down payment, but she's having trouble making the mortgage payments. One day she drives to Bryant's house and steals a briefcase containing twelve thousand dollars in cash. Twenty minutes later Bryant shows up at her house, crying and screaming that he needs the money. They talk. She agrees to keep two thousand and give him back the rest.

Also during this period Susan is dating Gordon, a state trooper who is a good counselor to her. Gordon is helping Susan to pull herself back together. She has not told him about the murders.

Chapter Eleven: THE CONFESSION

Dee is afraid that Bryant will murder her. She tells Susan, "If anything happens to me you go to the police." Susan points out that there is no proof that Bryant murdered Venecia. Susan talks Dee into writing a six-page confession. Dee does this in the presence of Susan and Jackie Ragan. Jackie, a waitress at IHOP, is Dee's friend and Dee has told her about the murders. Jackie has refused to hear anymore details and she walks out during the writing of the confession.

Jackie tells her roommate, Vicki, about the murders. Vicki calls the police.

In the meantime, Art Venecia's dog ran away on the night of the murder. Since then he has wandered in the nearby woods, refusing to come near people. But every night he comes to the house and whimpers on the lawn where the bodies are buried. Neighbors have called the police several times to report this. (The dog story, incidentally, ends happily when he is adopted by the new owner of the house.)

Chapter Twelve: THE ARRESTS

The police go to Richard Higgins, who has bought the house from Bryant (posing as Venecia). They ask permission to dig in his yard. They call the medical examiner. They dig up the bodies. Dee is arrested. (Susan gets word when her state trooper boyfriend calls her up and says "Your mother's been arrested for murder. What the hell is going on?") Bryant is arrested. He tells police that he was taken at knife point by the other three and forced to watch the murder of his lover. He says he went along with everything afterwards because he was afraid Dee would have him killed. Incredibly, the police let him go. (He is arrested again later.) Irvine is arrested. Rhodes, who has fled, is not arrested until much later when he is found hiding at his sister's house in Illinois.

Chapter Thirteen: THE TRIAL

Several months of pretrial planning, delays, etc. Dee's public defender, Art Koch, tries to use alcoholism as a defense, but the judge does not allow it. The four defendants are tried together. All except Bryant take the stand. At the trial Rhodes and Irvine say that they went to Venecia's house only to beat him up. They hit him over the head and knocked him out, they say, then they all left. But Bryant, they say, went back into the house, and, apparently, slit Venecia's throat at that time. The medical examiner's testimony seems to support this scenario, though it makes no difference in terms of Rhodes's and Irvine's guilt.

After five weeks they are found guilty of two murders and various other felonies. All four are sentenced to death. Judge Person takes notice of Dee, says that he sympathizes with her, but cannot in good conscience sentence the others to death, and not her.

EPILOGUE

Susan Garnet straightened herself out. Her boyfriend, Gordon, died of cancer at twenty-seven but was an inspiration to her. Her exposure to the criminal justice system, because of her mother, gave her career motivation. She is now a corrections officer at a prison in south Dade county. She underwent a religious conversion. She is closer to her mother than ever.

During her years in the county jail Dee has, of course, given up alcohol, and now she is always that nice sober person that Susan loved so much. In the county jail she established a community of friends, both inmates and employees, and has been doing social work within the jail. (As I write this she has only recently been transferred to death row at the state corrections facility in Pembroke and her adjustment will take time.) Her sentence is under appeal. Bryant, Irvine and Rhodes are all in state prison. The appeal of sentence could take several years.

THE SAMPLE CHAPTERS

With any proposal you should submit sample chapters, usually the first two if you're a beginner, and perhaps just the first chapter if you are established. Don't send an editor chapters nine and fifteen, or chapters four and twelve, just because you have more material on those and they are easier to write. An editor wants to experience a book the way a reader will, by reading from the first page.

The sample chapters are crucial. They show the editor how well you write and how you will approach your story. They should be as good as you can get them. Don't write something short and sketchy just to give the editor "an idea" of how they will go. Write and rewrite these sample chapters as if they were the final draft of the book. Certainly they will change by the time you finish the book, because you will have learned much more in your research. But, at the time of the proposal, the chapters should be your best work.

I'm not going to include the whole sample chapter from my *Delirium* proposal, but here are the first three pages, just to illustrate the point that a proposal should include a letter, an outline and sample chapters.

DELIRIUM
A True Story of Murder Under the Influence
By Gary Provost

CHAPTER ONE:

Dee Casteel was an ordinary woman. Everybody says so. Take Cally Maitlan, for example. For two years in the late 1970s Cally lived next door to Dee in South Miami. Their kids played together. Between loads of laundry Cally would visit at Dee's house. The women would talk and drink coffee, or sometimes Dee would sew. She was always good with her hands.

"We didn't talk about politics or philosophy or anything cerebral," says Cally, who is now an advertising copywriter but was then a mother and a housewife trying to make the best of things. "Just the kids and housework. The children were small then, and those were the things women talked about in those days. Dee worked as a waitress at the Saga Lounge, and she was a housewife. She kept the cleanest house I have ever seen. Dee and I were never really close, but I liked her a lot. She was always there with a favor, always anxious to help you out. After I moved away I never saw her again. But when I read in the papers that she had been sentenced to die in the electric chair I was shocked. Dee Casteel was the sweetest person you'd ever want to meet. It's so hard to believe she was involved in those murders."

The murders were committed in Dade County, Florida in the summer of 1983, and Dee Casteel was very much involved. People like Cally Maitlan learned very little about the murders from the newspaper. As bizarre as the murders were, the *Miami Herald* only ran a few small stories, perhaps because there were 545 other murders in Dade county that year.

The story of these murders begins on a Wednesday night in early June when Dee was working the three to eleven shift as a waitress at the International House of Pancakes on Route One in Naranja, about twenty miles south of downtown Miami.

When Dee saw Allen Bryant pull into the parking lot around ten that night she asked Jackie Ragan, the other waitress on duty, to watch her station while she rushed into the ladies' room to primp. Dee always liked to look her best when Allen was around. Other employees at the pancake house had noticed that whenever Allen entered a room Dee seemed to stand a little taller, smile a little more brightly, speak more slowly. Those who knew Dee well found this surprising, not because Dee was forty-six and Allen was twenty-six, but because Dee had always filled her life with large, stormy men, real macho numbers, and Allen was not only small, but gay. Allen, whose real name was James Allen Bryant, was the manager of the restaurant and for eight years he had been the lover of the restaurant's owner, Arthur Venecia. Venecia, who raised orchids and invested in the stock market, had bought the franchise specifically for Allen to manage.

In the ladies' room Dee coaxed her long dark hair into place, and pressed some fresh lipstick on her thin lips. She avoided a careful study of herself in the mirror. She knew she was gaunt these days. She had once been very pretty but she had squandered her good looks on alcohol, and she regretted that as much as anything. She checked her hands to be sure they were not shaking too badly. All day long she had been drinking vodka and coffee from a cup which she kept on the cook's counter.

When Dee emerged from the ladies' room Allen had already come into the restaurant. Wearing a blue boat-neck shirt and tight white jeans, he hovered over the cash register, and with frantic little motions of his long slender fingers he snatched bills out of the cash drawer as if he were snatching cheese from a mousetrap.

"Just getting some gas money," he said. "How's it going?" He gazed down into the cash drawer as if trying to decide how much more he should take.

A DIFFERENT KIND OF PROPOSAL

Just as a true crime book can be written many different ways, there is no one right way to write a proposal. What I've shown you is a fairly traditional, safe format for a proposal by a new writer. But you may feel that a different style of proposal is right for you or for your book. What follows is my proposal for a book called *Rich Blood*. As you will see, it is much less formal, much more conversational. The emphasis here is not on the structure of the book so much as it is on the elements of the book. This is much more like a sales pitch to the publisher. After you've established yourself as a true crime writer this might be the better way to write a proposal, since it can excite the editor about high points of a book and be flexible enough to let the editor get involved in shaping the book. For the beginner, however, this might be a more difficult way of selling a book, because the editor has no proof that you are capable of structuring the material.

One more point: There are probably many minor mistakes of fact in this proposal, as there will be in most true crime proposals. When you are at the early stages of investigating a story, you often are misinformed about names, dates and other details. This is not something to worry about, because nobody is going to publish the proposal, and you will certainly have all your facts straight by the time you write a final draft. However, in this case the proposal is going to be published, so I want to acknowledge that there may be a few factual errors.

And finally, even though I have not written *Rich Blood*, we can regard it as a successful proposal because I was offered substantial contracts to write it by a number of publishers. (I decided to write *Deadly Secrets* instead.)

We will, by the way, be discussing this proposal again later when we talk about plotting.

Dear Editor,

During the months since I finished writing my last true crime book I have considered several stories on which to base my next book. Many were strong, but until now I never had that jolt of enthusiasm, that certainty that I had gotten hold of a great human story that could sell a lot of books. *Rich Blood*, my proposed book, has great characters, millions of dollars, glamorous locales, celebrities, greed, fear, infidelity, family battles, a mother's love, a wife's anger and fear, a dogged and fascinating investigation by a determined police officer and prosecutor, a verdict that was always in doubt, and a jury decision that hung ultimately on something so small as a few fragments of tissue paper.

Most important, it's not a story about one freakish event by one bizarre person. It is a human story, with all the human emotions, and a central character with whom the reader can identify.

It is the kind of story that makes the reader ask: Given the same circumstances, would I have done the same thing? It is the story of Joyce Cohen.

Joyce Cohen was the poor little girl who grew up to marry a multimillionaire. She had achieved a great American dream, and when she saw that dream being snatched away from her she turned to a great American solution—murder.

An editorial in the *Miami Herald* put it this way: "As it turned out, the murder trial of Coconut Grove husband-killer Joyce Cohen was two stories in one. First, it was a personal saga of a woman married to a wealthy older man whom she didn't love, and who cheated on her. More broadly, it was the morality play of the 1980s Miami, of too much, too fast, too shallow."

This is not a story about a mass murderer or a raving psycho. It is a story about a person who strayed from the path of normal life, not someone who never walked the path in the first place. I've always been fascinated by what it is that turns apparently ordinary people to murder. I want to write about Joyce, one person who thought murder was an acceptable solution to her problems.

Joyce Cohen had a terrible childhood. Her mother was a prostitute, and her father was an alcoholic who sexually abused her. When her parents abandoned her she was brought up in foster homes. She grew up poor.

By the time Joyce was twenty-three she was bright, attractive and well liked. She was, according to her friends, a nice, friendly person who would hurt no one. She even became a foster parent to an under-privileged child overseas. By this time she was divorced after a short-lived marriage, and had one son, five-year-old Shawn. The future was not looking bright. Then she met Stanley Cohen. Joyce was a secretary. Stanley was a millionaire. His worth has been estimated at twelve million dollars, a fortune which he compiled as a builder of shopping malls in Florida. Joyce and Stanley fell in love, got married. Joyce was thrilled to have financial security and a rich father for her son. Stanley, twelve years older than Joyce, doted on his wife. He put her through design school and helped her build a career as an interior designer. (Joyce dabbled in other business ventures. At the time of the murder she was trying to market a headband with an ice pack to keep people cool during exercise.) He adopted her son. He gave her nice, expensive things. He built a house for her on his six-hundred-acre ranch in Steamboat Springs, Colorado. They lived the lifestyles of the rich and famous in Coconut Grove, Florida, and often flew in Stanley's private jet to Steamboat Springs, the ski resort, where Joyce soon was living the high life with the likes of Tanya Tucker. Joyce grew to like the jet set life. She liked spending money, meeting celebrities. The ordinary secretary had scored big. She had money, rich friends, expensive clothes. And then she saw the possibility of it all being taken away.

The marriage grew cold. Joyce was young and vibrant. Her husband had been handsome and lively, but after his heart attack he was not quite so youthful. Joyce told friends that Stanley no longer looked as good, no longer dressed so nicely. Joyce tired of her husband, and he tired of her. For the last two years of their marriage they had no sex. Joyce was in constant conflict with Stanley's two children by a previous marriage: Gary, the up-and-coming lawyer, and Gerri, the well-known Miami television news anchorwoman. Joyce and Stanley fought. She wanted out of the marriage. "You can leave," he told her, "but you'll leave this marriage the way you came into it. Broke."

Joyce had a horror of ever being poor again; she could not bear it. She confessed to friends that she was afraid that she would be left penniless, that the court would look at her newfound reputation for high living and would give her nothing. She told Tanya Tucker her concerns about money. She worried out loud that her stepchildren would inherit her husband's fortune and said that her son, Shawn, deserved to be the heir.

By 1985 the marriage was in serious crisis. At a Coconut Grove restaurant owned by her husband, Joyce met a man named Lynn Barkley and began having an affair with him. Stanley, meanwhile, was having an affair with his old flame, Carol Hughes, a junior high school art teacher, whom he had almost married in 1972. Joyce found out about the affair. She was enraged and frightened. Carol was a threat. It was all becoming clear to Joyce. Stanley would leave her for this other woman and he would leave Joyce without a cent. She would be poor again. No more cocaine. No more jetting to Colorado. No more rich and famous friends.

On March 7, 1986, while Stanley Cohen was sleeping in his Coconut Grove house, (just three weeks before his daughter's wedding) he was shot four times in the head. Joyce called the police. She told them that at 5 A.M. she had been on the phone talking to one of her Colorado friends when she heard a shot. She ran upstairs. There was Stanley, dead, blood all over the pillow. She heard someone run out the door.

It was a plausible enough story but the police sensed that something wasn't right. Why had the burglar alarm been shut off? Why had the Doberman, Mischief, been locked up? Why did Joyce seem reluctant to have them look around? The police suspected that Joyce was involved in her husband's murder.

A week later police arrested Frank Zucarello, a good looking, twenty-five-year-old waiter, who was charged with several burglaries. Zucarello, who is what police call a "home invasion specialist," made a deal; for a reduced sentence he would tell what he knew about the Stanley Cohen murder. He said that he and Anthony Caracciolo and another man met with Joyce Cohen at a convenience store in North Miami Beach, along with Lynn Barkley, the nightclub owner with whom Joyce was having the affair. Joyce, Zucarello said, hired them to fake a burglary at her house and kill Stanley Cohen. On the night of the murder it was Joyce who let the men in. "Hurry up, get it over with," she told them. It was Caracciolo who pulled the trigger.

The state prosecutor's office was now sure that Joyce had played a part in her husband's murder, but felt there was not enough evidence to go to trial with. The rumors began. Joyce was whispered about all through Coconut Grove society and all over Miami. She murdered her husband, people said. Still, there was no arrest.

Joyce and her son moved to Chesapeake, Virginia. She found a new boyfriend. They made plans for marriage. Joyce worked at a children's hospital. She picked vegetables from her fiancé's garden and gave them to the elderly.

Meanwhile, in Miami, the investigation continued for three

years. The children of Stanley Cohen, seeking both justice for their father and the twelve million dollars which now had gone to Joyce kept pressure on the state's attorney. Finally, three weeks ago, Joyce Cohen was brought to trial for the first-degree murder of her husband.

I had heard about the story when I was in Florida. I then went to Texas, where the story haunted me. I knew this was the story for me, so I flew back to Miami to catch the end of the trial.

Joyce, free on one million dollars bail, wore wide rimmed glasses that she had never worn before. She wore conservative dresses. Obviously, she had been coached by her charismatic lawyer, Alan Ross. She cried often. Three of her female friends sat behind her, whispering their support. Sitting behind them were Gary and Gerri, and (in a wheelchair) Stanley's brother Arthur and other members of the family. They came every day, looking for justice. They wanted their stepmother, now thirty-nine, to burn in the electric chair for murdering their father.

Zucarello testified. (The other two killers have not been tried yet. I will go to their trials as part of my research for this book.) He told his story about the meeting at the convenience store, about being given a map of the house, about the murder. Zucarello's testimony, however, was probably not the thing that swayed the jury. He was, after all, making a sweet deal for himself. Facing several life sentences, he had negotiated a deal whereby he ended up getting five years, plus probation. (One of the subplots in this book will be the way these questionable deals are made that allow professional criminals to testify at many trials and go virtually unpunished for their own crimes. Zucarello, for example, talked about how the police took him out for a haircut when he was in custody and let him visit his girlfriend's house where he had sex with her while the police waited for him.)

The jury almost certainly was convinced by some fascinating and highly detailed scientific evidence which had accumulated during the investigation.

The trial was dramatic. It had all the elements of television and movie trials, those things that I'm always telling people "don't happen in real life." This time they happened in real life.

The medical examiner, Charles Wetli, said that Stanley Cohen had died between 2 and 3 A.M., three hours before Joyce called the police. This was a shocker, because he had originally concluded a time of death that was consistent with Joyce's story. (It's too much to go into here, but there's a lot of very intriguing testimony concerning exact times, phone calls, clocks, etc. At one point in the trial, the prosecutor pointed out that even if we accept Joyce's version of events, five minutes went by between the phone conversation she was having when she claims to have heard the shots, and her call to 911. For dramatic effect he sat down and remained silent for five full minutes to demonstrate just how much time that was to delay a call to police when you've just found your husband murdered.)

Most significantly, an expert testified about minute particles of tissue that were found on the gun. The tissue matched tissue found in Joyce Cohen's wastebasket, a tissue which also contained traces of her mucus. Furthermore, traces of gunpowder had been found on the tissue and on Joyce's hands. As the prosecutor, Kevin DiGregory, saw it, the killers had panicked and left the gun behind. Joyce had then wiped it off with a tissue and tossed it in some shrubbery in the yard, where it was later found. DiGregory told the jury, "If Joyce Cohen handled that gun, then she's guilty."

The point was so crucial that the jury, during its deliberations, asked to hear the scientific testimony read back to them.

While the jury was out I spoke to a number of lawyers and asked them what they thought the verdict would be. She'll be acquitted, they said, there's too much room for reasonable doubt. Even Stanley Cohen's kids, filled with hatred for Joyce, believed she would get off.

Since this was a trial of surprises and uncertainty I want to bring the trial into the book, as I did with *Fatal Dosage*.

The jury deliberated for two days. Two weeks ago they came in with a verdict. A few days later Joyce Cohen was sentenced to life in prison without the possibility of parole for forty years.

I'm convinced that this story has the basic elements that make for a good true crime book.

1. *Fascinating characters*
- Joyce, the poor girl who married rich and was so afraid of being poor again that she turned to murder.
- Stanley Cohen, the millionaire mall builder. Was he the saint that his children remember, or was he the bastard that others claim?
- The victim's son, a rising young attorney.
- The victim's daughter, a local television personality.
- Joyce's lawyer, well known, glamorous.
- Tanya Tucker, the famous country-western singer.
- Kevin DiGregory, the determined prosecutor.
- Jon Spear, the homicide detective who stuck to the case until it was solved.

- Wetli, the medical examiner.
- Zucarello, Caracciolo, and Thomas Lamberti, the "home invasion specialists," called "the bungling burglars" because they had once broken into a house next door to the one they were supposed to be hitting.
- Carol Hughes, the art teacher who had almost married the millionaire, and was having an affair with him when he died.
- Lynn Barkley, who allegedly was in on the conspiracy, but has never been charged.
- Joyce's friends, the rich ladies who testified for her and claimed that Stanley's life was being threatened by someone else, that he was connected to a well-known fugitive dope-dealing lawyer.

2. *A sense of place.*

We have Coconut Grove, which arguably, is the most desirable place to live in the Miami area. Chic, affluent, artistic, it is the kind of place that readers want to visit vicariously. And we have Steamboat Springs, Colorado, a ski resort for the rich and famous, another great fantasy trip for readers who want their characters bigger than life. All of this in contrast to Joyce's impoverished childhood in Carpentersville, Illinois.

3. *Uncertainty.*

This book will be filled with compelling narrative questions every step of the way, right up to the verdict.

Of course it is impossible for any writer to say for sure what the shape of his book will be, until after he has done all the research. But as I envision the book now, I think the construction that is most compelling and has maximum impact would be something like this:

1. The crime, from the police perspective. What seems to have occurred. The police begin to doubt Joyce and start to investigate.

2. The investigation.

3. Who is this woman they are investigating? Joyce's childhood, the years with Stanley, the high living. The circumstances that might have brought her to murder.

4. Joyce's new life in Virginia, interrupted by:

5. The indictment. After three years prosecutors think they have enough to convict.

6. The trial.

I believe the story as I've told it here could make for a compelling and popular book. But there is another dimension to all of this, an important twist.

Joyce Cohen might not be guilty.

If I were on the Cohen jury I certainly would have voted for acquittal, because there is a good deal of room for reasonable doubt. But there is more room for doubt than even the jurors knew.

Consider this:

1. After the murder Joyce passed two different polygraph tests, answering questions presented by the police. The tests were given on different days by different examiners. One of the polygraph examiners is the best in the state, a man used often by the state's attorney's office and the police. (The jury was never told about the lie detector tests.)

2. One of Joyce's friends says that a week before Stanley Cohen was murdered, he told employees that his life had been threatened and, the friend says, Stanley was urging Joyce to keep the doors locked at work.

3. Stanley Cohen was alleged to be friendly with a well-known Miami attorney who, accused of drug dealing, is now a fugitive from justice.

4. According to police, Stanley Cohen received a mysterious visit from a Miami underworld figure at 1:30 in the morning, two nights before he was murdered.

5. For three years the medical examiner said that Stanley Cohen's time of death was consistent with Joyce's story. Only on the eve of the trial did the M.E. change his opinion.

6. Do Joyce's alleged statements about being left penniless make sense? She was married to the man for twelve years, and Florida has an equal distribution law. Why would she expect to be left without money?

7. Stanley Cohen was disliked by many people. People other than Joyce, it would seem, had motives for murder.

8. Stanley Cohen was killed with his own gun. But does this make sense? Home invasion specialists can get guns easily enough. Why would Joyce have them, very suspiciously, use Stanley's gun? If she did wait three hours to call the police, then why all the alleged frantic activity . . . tossing the gun out, etc. In three hours she could very carefully cover her tracks.

All of which leads to an alternative scenario:

Maybe Joyce didn't kill her husband. Maybe one of his enemies did. Maybe Stanley's kids believe she did it, or in any case maybe they don't want to see the millions going to her. Maybe the state's attorney's office is influenced by the fact that the family is connected to the media. Maybe Zucarello senses the pressure on police to solve the Cohen case. Maybe he tells them what they want to hear, in exchange for the immunity he got.

Maybe an innocent woman is in prison.

My approach to writing a true crime is to find the natural story in the material and fortify it with a lot of strong narrative questions which are paid off along the way, just as a compelling novel is. I also like to give the reader room for his own conclusions and discussions. In this book, *the reader will know a lot more than the jury did, and can come to a more informed conclusion about Joyce's guilt or innocence.*

One way of looking at the narrative questions and the payoffs, the twists in the story, is as a series of "buts." Of course, I will discover most of the "buts" when I get into researching and writing the book. For now, here are a few:

Joyce is a poor secretary, but she meets a millionaire and marries him.

She's married to a millionaire, but the marriage goes sour.

She wants to end the marriage, but she (allegedly) thinks she'll be left penniless.

She perhaps has a motive for murdering her husband, but so do other people.

After the murder, police suspect her, but she passes two polygraph exams by two different examiners at two different times and places. One, a highly regarded expert.

She passes the polygraphs, but the court rules they will not be allowed. But a federal court rules in a different case that the polygraphs can be allowed.

She goes back to court to get the polygraph tests allowed, but Judge Smith still will not allow them.

Someone claims to have heard shots at 3:30 A.M., but the medical examiner says that Stanley died around 5:30 A.M., consistent with Joyce's story. She seems to be telling the truth, but it was five minutes from the time of the Colorado phone call to the call to 911.

Joyce allegedly says to Officer Catherine Parker "I shouldn't have done it," but Parker never reports this.

Three days after the murder a cop tells the medical examiner that he saw signs of lividity, indicating that the body had been dead for a few hours. But Wetli, the medical examiner, reviews his material, still comes to same conclusion. Stays with that conclusion for three years.

No charges against Joyce, but the *Miami Herald* starts an anti-Joyce campaign, demanding that she be brought to justice.

Newscaster Gerri Helfman is about to get married, but her father is murdered.

No charges are brought against Joyce, but Stanley's family pressures the state's attorney's office to come up with something.

The case is apparently going nowhere, but the police arrest Zucarello, and he says he was in on the Cohen murder. But he's bargaining to get out of eleven life sentences, the state's attorney's office is anxious for a break in the case, and an incredibly sweet deal is made.

(Notes on home invasion specialists. They would disguise themselves as postmen, flower delivery men, even police officers to get into houses, tie people up, rob them.)

Zucarello says he has two accomplices, but the police can't find them.

Joyce is apparently free of prosecution now and she is rich, but the Cohen children file a civil suit, claiming she was responsible for the murder, and the money is tied up in civil court. Now Joyce is broke.

She is broke and an unhappy widow in Virginia, but she meets a man and falls in love.

Police come up with some scientific evidence that might implicate Joyce, but it's not enough for an indictment.

Police have two suspects, but they can't find them. (After eighteen months they find one, eight months later they find the other.) There is not enough evidence for the state's attorney's office, but one of the family members pressing for an indictment is a well-known newscaster whose goodwill can be politically advantageous.

Zucarello might not have been at the house. He might be lying, but he knows that one of the four shots missed Stanley, and that was never in the paper. But the police might have supplied him with that information.

Joyce is living a normal life in Virginia, but she is indicted for the murder of her husband.

She is indicted, but nobody thinks she'll be convicted, even her enemies. (They come to trial every day.)

The medical examiner testifies, but suddenly changes his opinion, now says that Cohen had been dead for a few hours.

The state wants Joyce's son as witness, DiGregory goes to Virginia to videotape him, but they decide not to use it.

It seems clear that there is reasonable doubt, but the jury finds her guilty.

She could get the death penalty, but the sentence is life.

Final reader question: Did she do it?

Thanks for reading.

Sincerely,

Gary Provost

SOURCES

When you write a book proposal you certainly don't know what all of your sources of information will be. But there are many that you can anticipate, and if you include them in your proposal, your project will certainly seem a lot more credible.

Here is a list of sources, as I presented it in my *Delirium* proposal. As it turned out, there were several people on the list whom I never talked to. But of course there were many more not on the list, who did contribute to my knowledge of the story. Your sources list, like your outline, only reflects your *intention* at the time of the proposal. No one can predict what will happen when you get into really researching and writing the book.

DELIRIUM
A True Story of Murder Under the Influence
By Gary Provost

PARTIAL LIST OF SOURCES:
Dee Casteel
Susan Garnet
Michael Irvine
James Allen Bryant (possibly)
William Rhodes (possibly)
Art Koch, Dee's lawyer
Jeff Shapiro, Bryant's lawyer
Howard Sohn, Irvine's lawyer
Jackie Ragan, Dee's friend

Cally Maitlan, and various acquaintances of Dee Casteel
Sally Weintraub, prosecuting attorney
Jay Novick, prosecuting attorney
Robert Yappell, owner of the Amoco station where Irvine and Rhodes
     worked as mechanics
Paula Cook, sister of William Rhodes
Felix Santos, and various friends of Allen Bryant
Chip Jenkins, backhoe operator
Trial transcript
Court file
Defendants' statements to police
Depositions of Susan Garnet, Jackie Ragan, Richard Higgins, Sandra
     Lochard, Bill Sussman and others who were present during sales of
     property
Reid Welch and various friends, relatives and acquaintances of Arthur
     Venecia
Detectives Kenneth Meyer, Alejandro Alvarez, and about a dozen
     other detectives with the Miami-Dade Metro police
Interviews with some of the twenty-nine witnesses called by the state
Jean Kirkpatrick, Executive Director, Women for Sobriety, and
     various experts and literature on alcoholism
Various literature on women drawn to destructive relationships,
     Women Who Love Too Much, et al.
"The Corpse Had a Familiar Face," by Edna Buchanan, and various
     literature on crime in Miami.

GETTING A CONTRACT

This is a book about writing a true crime, not about getting published
in general, so I can't cover everything about the process of getting a
contract for your proposed true crime book. I will, however, give you
the condensed version and a few tips for finding out more.

Your proposal will arrive on an editor's desk either directly from
you, or from a literary agent.

If you are going to send the proposal directly to a publisher you
will need to know which publishers are appropriate. You don't want
to send your true crime proposal to a house that only puts out books
on orchid growing and greyhound racing.

You can find appropriate publishers for your true crime book
listed in *Writer's Market* (Writer's Digest Books, 1507 Dana Avenue,

Cincinnati, OH 45207), *Literary Market Place* (R.R. Bowker, 245 West 17th Street, New York, NY 10011), and *The Insider's Guide to Book Editors and Publishers* (Prima Publishing and Communications, P.O. Box 1260JH, Rocklin, CA 95677).

Whenever you send anything to a book publisher you want to send it to a specific editor. Don't send it simply to the publisher. If you do that it will end up in the slush pile and nobody will take it seriously. You can find the names of editors in the books I've mentioned. Also if you read the acknowledgment sections of several true crime books you will find that authors often thank their editors. That will give you the names of some editors who have bought true crime books. If you come upon a true crime book that seems to be the sort of thing you would like to write, call the publisher, ask for the editorial department, and ask who was the editor for that book.

Here is a list of book editors who specifically mentioned an interest in true crime in *The Insider's Guide to Book Editors and Publishers*. This is only a sampling. In that directory, and the others, you will find dozens of editors who are interested in receiving true crime proposals, though it might not be specifically mentioned in their listing.

Ann Godoff, Senior Editor
The Atlantic Monthly Press
19 Union Square West
New York, New York 10003

Daniel Zitin, Executive Editor
Fawcett Books
201 E. 50th Street
New York, New York 10022

Kate Miciak, Senior Editor
Bantam Books
666 Fifth Avenue
New York, New York 10103

Jane Rosenman, Editor
Delacorte Press
666 Fifth Avenue
New York, New York 10103

David Gibbons, Associate Editor
Donald I. Fine, Inc.
19 W. 21st Street
New York, New York 10010

Gladys Justin Carr, Vice President
Harper and Row, Inc.
10 E. 53rd Street
New York, New York 10022

Thomas W. Miller, Senior Editor
(same as above)

Craig Nelson, Senior Editor
(same as above)

Lisa Drew, Senior Editor
William Morrow and Co.
105 Madison Avenue
New York, New York 10016

Ms. Michaela Hamilton, Executive Editor
New American Library
1633 Broadway
New York, New York 10019

Pamela Dorman, Senior Editor
Penguin USA
40 W. 23rd Street
New York, New York 10010

Lisa Kaufman, Editor
(same as above)

Maria Arana-Ward, Vice President
Simon and Schuster
1230 Avenue of the Americas
New York, New York 10020

Rick Horgan, Senior Editor
Warner Books, Inc.
666 Fifth Avenue
New York, New York 10103

Of course, if you engage a literary agent you won't be sending anything directly to these or any other editors. Your agent will do that.

In order to get an agent for your true crime book proposal you should do the following:

1. Write a fabulous true crime book proposal.

2. Send a self-addressed stamped envelope to each of these organizations and ask for a list of their member agents. These will all be legitimate, reliable agents, not snake oil salesmen. This is important,

because there are a lot of fools out there passing themselves off as agents who have no business doing so.

Independent Literary Agents Association, Inc.
% Ellen Levine Literary Agency
432 Park Avenue S. #1205
New York, New York 10016

Society of Author's Representatives, Inc.
10 Astor Place, 3rd Floor
New York, New York 10003

(Incidentally, you can also find lists of agents in the three directories I mentioned earlier.)

3. Send the proposal to any agent who asks to see it, but only to *one agent at a time*. Don't worry that agent number two is going to get impatient during the several weeks it will take agent one to make a decision. Several weeks in agent time is like a few days to most of us.

4. Once an agent has agreed to represent your book, meet with him or her or at least have a long telephone call to convince yourself that this is a person you want to get hooked up with.

5. To learn all about agents, so that you will be able to carry on intelligent conversations, read *How to Be Your Own Literary Agent* by Richard Curtis (Houghton Mifflin), *The Literary Agent and the Writer* by Diane Cleaver (The Writer, Inc.), or *Literary Agents: How to Get and Work with the Right One for You* (Writer's Digest Books).

How Much Money?

Even though this is not a book about publishing in general, I will go into a bit of detail on this important subject, mainly because I know it is maddening to read about how to write anything and not have some sense of how much money one gets paid for writing it.

True crimes are published as original paperbacks and as hardcovers, which often are later reprinted as paperbacks.

There is no clear-cut rule about which true crimes should be published in hardcover and which in paperback, though you will hear editors talk about "up market" (well-heeled characters, large themes, high profile cases) and "down market" (graphic murders, heavy violence, tabloid material) books. Really, each book must be judged on its own merits and circumstances. My book, *Across the Border*, for example, was published in paperback because the publisher felt there was a high interest level in the material, but one that might not last long, and the mass market paperback was the best way to get a lot of copies out quickly.

For an original paperback you will probably get an advance somewhere in the range of $10,000-$20,000, and a royalty rate of 6 to 10 percent of the cover price of the book. The advance is an amount of money that is advanced to you from the expected royalties. Typically you will get half of it when you sign the contract and the other half when you deliver a satisfactory manuscript.

If your book is to be published in hardcover you might get an advance of $10,000, but it can go as high as $50,000 or even $100,000 if your proposal excites more than one publisher. If your hardcover publisher later sells the reprint rights to a paperback publisher you will, generally, get half of whatever the hardcover publisher receives.

It seems to me that the best deal you can make these days, though, is something called the hard-soft deal. In this arrangement one publisher buys both hardcover and softcover rights. You get one advance, larger than what you would have gotten for just hard or soft rights. When the paperback comes out you get all of the royalties instead of just half. And, perhaps most important, your hardcover is being published by a company that knows it's going to be trying to sell the same book in paperback a year later, and so has a long-term interest in supporting the book.

If you want to learn more about book contracts and publishing in general, I recommend *The Freelance Writer's Handbook* (New American Library), mainly because I wrote it; *Beyond the Best Seller List* by Richard Curtis (Houghton Mifflin); and the many fine books on publishing that are offered by Writer's Digest Books.

4

GATHERING INFORMATION

While I was writing this I heard about a case in California that attracted me. Michael Blatt, who had been the general manager of the Seattle Seahawks football team had been fired. Allegedly, he had then hired two ex-football players to kill Lawrence Carnegie, the California man whom Blatt, allegedly, believed was responsible for his firing. The two men allegedly murdered Carnegie with a bow and arrow.

The story had many fine ingredients. The accused is a millionaire, a good looking young man whom everybody says "couldn't possibly have done it." The victim, apparently, had nothing to do with the man's firing. Then there were the two black ex-football players. Had their desire to play football been exploited by the man who allegedly hired them, I wondered. There was the bow and arrow, of course. And the intriguing world of professional football.

Last night about six o'clock (here on the east coast) I got on the phone. I wanted to track down more information. All I had on my notepad were the names of the accused, the victim and his wife, Karen, and the fact that Blatt had been general manager of the Seahawks, along with the words "trial in Waukeen, California," which was my phonetic spelling of what I assumed would turn out to be Joaquin, because I thought I had heard of a Joaquin, California.

My goal was to get news clippings about the story so that I would know more, and to contact Karen Carnegie to see if she would cooperate with me if I decided to write a book about the murder.

Here are the phone calls I made:

1. *To an operator to get an area code for Seattle, Washington.*

2. *To Seattle information for the number of the public library.*

3. *To the Seattle public library.* I told them I wanted someone who could pull newspaper clippings on the story for me. They told me I needed the government and public affairs division and gave me the phone number for that division.

4. *To the government and public affairs division of the Seattle public library.* I asked the librarian if he had anything on file on the Blatt case. He punched a few keys on his computer and reported to me the headlines, dates and page numbers for stories appearing in the *Seattle Times.* I asked him if I could get copies of the stories. He said yes, if I put in a request at my local library.

5. *To long-distance information in California.* I asked for an area code for Joaquin, California. The operator had no Joaquin, but she did have a San Joaquin.

6. *To San Joaquin information.* I asked for the number of the San Joaquin public library.

7. *To the San Joaquin public library.* I asked the librarian if she could do some research on the case for me. She had never heard of the case. Perhaps I was thinking of San Joaquin City, she said. It was a totally different place, she said. It was up around Sacramento, she said.

8. *To the Sacramento area information operator.* I asked for San Joaquin City. No such place, she said. But there was a San Juan City. Perhaps I was thinking of that, she said. No, I said.

I checked my encyclopedia and could find no city of Joaquin, but there was a San Joaquin County. Perhaps the city I wanted was in San Joaquin County. But who would know where this guy Blatt was being held? Well, he was a former general manager of a professional football team. The sportswriters in his city would certainly follow the story.

9. *To Seattle information.* I asked for the number of the *Seattle Times.*

10. *To the* Seattle Times. I asked for the sports department. When someone answered I asked him if he knew where Blatt was being tried for murder. Stockton, California, he told me. I checked my map and saw that Stockton was in San Joaquin County.

11. *To Stockton information for the number of the Stockton public library.*

12. *To the Stockton public library.* I asked them if they could do some research on the case. They said they weren't equipped for extensive research but they would photocopy three or four stories about the case and send them to me. It would take about three days.

13. *To Stockton information.* I asked if they had a number for Karen Carnegie, the widow of the victim. They gave me a number.

14. *To the Stockton number.* It turned out to be the number of a real estate firm which had been owned by Karen and Lawrence Carnegie, but which she had since sold. The man on the phone gave me a new number for Karen Carnegie.

15. *To the new number for Karen Carnegie.* It was her employer, and she was out of the office. I left my name and number.

I could have made calls all night. But I stopped at this point. After all, I was only gathering information to decide if I wanted to write a book on the murder.

Karen Carnegie called me this morning. I told her I was thinking about writing a book about her husband's murder and wanted to know if she would give me an interview. She told me her late husband's family had decided not to talk to any writers or reporters, and that she would go along with their wishes.

All that, just to get a few newspaper clippings and to find out that one person would not talk to me about a book, which I probably won't even write.

I've described this little phone session for you because it is typical. When the true crime writer begins to investigate a story he does not have any magical secrets or special connections to information. He simply picks up the phone and calls information. He calls wrong numbers, wrong places and right places at wrong times. But he just keeps dialing. As I said earlier, it all begins with the names you got from your first story about the crime. At the beginning there is usually no systematic master plan for gathering information. One call, simply, leads to another.

Whenever I do this I am reminded of a conversation I once had with Justin Kaplan, the Pulitzer Prize–winning biographer. I asked Kaplan how a biographer finds out where the various letters and papers of his intended subject are located, and how he finds out who the experts on the subject are.

"Oh, there are all sorts of academic journals that list that sort of thing," he said.

"Can you give me some examples?" I said.

"No," Kaplan said. "I don't use them. I just ask around."

That's what the true crime writer does. He just asks around.

On Paths

I find it useful to view my investigation in terms of paths. In the example above I pursued a "Seattle path," and a "California path." If I were to pursue the story further I would go deeper down the Seattle path by calling the Seattle Seahawks for information. Soon I would discover new paths. I might find, for example, that Blatt grew up in Oklahoma and that would lead me to an "Oklahoma path," or that he was a roller skating champion and that would place me at the beginning of a "roller skating path."

Of course this idea of paths is just one way of looking at the process and it might not be helpful to you. But I find it useful because often one path will reveal information that was denied to me on another. For example, let's say my goal is to talk to Blatt's friends. On my Seattle path I might call the Seahawks and find that none of his friends there will talk to the press because they're afraid they'll get fired. So I ask myself, where would I find friends of Blatt whose jobs are not in jeopardy. The answer is, on the roller skating path. So I call the roller rink where Blatt skated and I ask for the names of some of his roller skating pals. And so forth.

From Newspapers

In the Blatt example, you'll note that my main goal when I first started snooping was to get some newspaper clippings about the case. I like to gather as much as I can. This gives me the basic story, along with names, dates and places.

Newspaper stories by themselves are of limited value, because they almost always have mistakes in them, and until you investigate further you have no way of knowing what the mistakes are. So, generally, don't include in your book information that is just a rewrite of information you found in a newspaper, unless you have verified it from other sources.

However, newspapers are a great place to discover more reliable sources. A story might tell you the name of the criminal's hometown, the name of his lawyer, his employer, the court he was tried in, the prosecutor on the case, the names of witnesses against him, even his home address. Go from there. In other words, don't use newspaper stories as sources unless you absolutely have to; *use them to find sources.*

With the book *Without Mercy*, the only news clipping I ever needed was the first one. I gathered others, but they turned out to be unnecessary, because my interview subjects led me to my sources. When I wrote *Across the Border* I was much more dependent on newspaper clippings because I had less than three months to write the book, so a lot of what I wrote was based strictly on news reports. However, I verified as much of it as possible with interviews, and, as usual, I found that very few news reports were 100 percent accurate.

Getting Newspaper Clippings. Most stories have one center. The satanic cult story had its center in Brownsville, Texas. (Actually the center was across the river in Matamoros, Mexico, but I'm looking at it from the perspective of a person who can't read Spanish language newspapers.)

Some stories have more than one center. If the lieutenant governor of Wisconsin goes to Little Rock and bludgeons to death the governor of Arkansas, then Arkansas is the center for a story called "Governor Slain by Disgruntled Wisconsin Politician," and Wisconsin is the center for a story called "Lieutenant Governor Goes Crazy, Murders Arkansas Governor."

In any case a news story is like a rock being thrown into a placid pond. It sends ripples outward and those ripples get weaker as they get farther from the center. So even though a well-publicized case might spawn wire service stories that appear all over the country, and an article in *People Weekly* magazine, your best source of news stories is at the center.

A CASE HISTORY

Because *Across the Border* is the book of mine that was most dependent on news clippings, I'll use that as the example to show you how you might acquire newspaper stories.

When Pocket Books asked me to write a book about the cult killings in Mexico, it happened that I was on my way to Texas anyway, where I was to speak at a writer's conference in Longview. After my Longview date I drove the 500 miles south to Brownsville. Along the way on a Sunday afternoon, April 23, I stopped in Houston at the main library downtown. (I find that most big city libraries keep at least the main library open on Sundays; after all, that's when college students need them most.)

Libraries are the repositories for local newspapers. (The newspaper offices, of course, keep the papers on file, but they rarely let outsiders use their library.) All libraries will keep the local newspaper on file, either in stacks on a shelf or indexed on microfilm. Medium sized libraries will have the local newspaper, newspapers from big cities in the region, the *New York Times* on microfilm, and maybe a few of the major newspapers from around the country, such as the *Washington*

Post and the *Los Angeles Times*. (Libraries will often subscribe also to a newspaper of special interest to its community. Even a small library in a community with a large Jewish population, for example, might get a Tel Aviv newspaper.)

Big city libraries will have all of the above and the daily, or Sunday edition of perhaps a few dozen newspapers from major cities around the country and around the world. While the *New York Times* is almost always on microfilm, the others will usually be actual newspapers in the newspaper room or stacked in a closet at the top of a long stairway.

"So Gary," you're asking, "how come you didn't just pull the Houston and Dallas newspapers at the Boston public library, an hour from your home?"

The answer is that out-of-town newspapers are sent to libraries, apparently, by mule train. The libraries are usually two or three weeks behind on newspapers that come from more than two states away. The newspapers I read in Houston hadn't even arrived in Boston.

So, getting back to Houston. I stopped at the downtown library, knowing that I would find the Houston, Dallas, San Antonio and Austin newspapers there. I also knew that the major Texas newspapers would have a lot more about the crimes than my newspapers back in New England. Of course, Texas papers would have the same UPI and AP wire service stories as the Boston papers, but because this was a Texas story each of those newspapers would also have sent its own reporters.

Since the Houston and Dallas newspapers were not indexed at the Houston library it was important that I know the dates I was looking for. If you go to the library and tell the librarian you want the newspapers covering a story that happened, "Sometime last year," she's going to give you a look that would peel the paint off a new car, and then she's going to take you into a back room and sit you down in front of a stack of newspapers that is six times your own height. Your fingers will be black with ink and your eyes red with eyestrain long before you find what you're looking for. In other words, get some dates before you go to the library.

Mark Kilroy had disappeared in the early morning hours of March 14, and the bodies at the Santa Elena ranch were discovered on April 9. In Houston I asked the librarian to fetch me all the Dallas and Houston newspapers for March 14, 15 and 16, and all the papers from April 9 to the present.

I didn't expect to find much of anything in the March papers.

The disappearance of Mark Kilroy had been a big story in Brownsville, but it was certainly not big enough to make much of a ripple in Dallas or Houston. I also didn't expect to find much in the newspapers of April 9, the day the bodies were discovered, because the story wouldn't normally make it into print until the following day. But I was being careful. There was always the chance that the story had made it into an evening edition on the ninth.

I spent that Sunday afternoon in the Houston library, photocopying every story I could find that was related to the case. It's important to take a broad view of that term "related to the case." A big story spawns many smaller stories, and all of them can enrich your book. When I left the Houston library that day I had the basic coverage of the discovery of the bodies on the ranch. I also had stories about Mark Kilroy's friends mourning him in his hometown, a story about the drug problem along the border, stories about Mexican-American relations, editorials on satanism, interviews with experts on Afro-Caribbean religions, a story about the role of the U.S. Customs Service in the case, and a few dozen other stories.

When I got to Brownsville, Texas, I took a slightly different approach. I knew there would be stories about the case in virtually every edition of the *Brownsville Herald* from the time Mark Kilroy disappeared until the present, which was April 25. I knew that with two or three stories in each edition published after the discovery, I would have to put five or six quarters into the photocopy machine for each newspaper I drew from, and that I would spend hours looking for the stories, folding pages to photocopy, waiting for the photocopy machine to be available, searching for change, waiting for somebody to fix the photocopy machine which would, undoubtedly, break, waiting for someone to finish reading one of the papers I needed, and putting the papers back in order. There was a simpler, faster, cheaper way to get my stories. I drove to the office of the *Brownsville Herald* and for about twenty bucks I bought a copy of every issue of the paper published since March 14.

"Wait a minute, Gary," you're saying. "Why didn't you buy all the Houston papers when you were in Houston?"

It was Sunday. The newspaper office was closed.

After I left Matamoros and Brownsville I drove to Dallas, where I would get my flight back to Boston. While in Dallas I used the library in a slightly different way to get news stories. I put in a request for a computer search of the Dallas newspapers between April 25 and the present, which by then was May 2. I gave the librarian certain key words such as "Constanzo," "Matamoros" and "satanism." Four days later there arrived at my house, along with a reasonable bill for services, a computer printout of all the Dallas newspaper stories published during those dates and indexed under those headings.

While I was in Brownsville and Matamoros, the cult story had not yet found its natural ending. That is, I didn't know how my book would end. Adolfo Constanzo, leader of the cult, and Sara Aldrete, the so-called "witch" of the cult, were still at large, along with several other cult members.

By May 10, when the missing cult members were captured or killed in a four-hour Mexico City shootout, I was back home in Massachusetts working on the book. Now it was time to use my local library.

At the libraries in my area I was able to keep in touch with the story by periodically reading the Texas newspapers. At the Boston public library I was able to get *The News*, an English language newspaper published in Mexico City, which covered the shootout extensively.

Later, when we talk about techniques of writing the true crime I'll show you how some of the newspaper material showed up in the published book. But, for now, there is one other point I want to make about newspaper clippings. That is, don't read the newspapers just for the facts concerning your case; read them also for the "sense of time" and "sense of place," which will be part of your book. What else was going on in the world when the events of your story were unfolding? What stories were typical of your place? Later, I'll give you examples of how these things can enrich your book.

THE COURT FILE

As a case moves from arrest to trial it generates a good deal of paperwork. There are depositions, search warrants, letters, police reports and various bits of evidence in written form. Much of this will end up in the court file long before the trial. This file is public record and it grows fatter as the months go by and as the judge on the case allows materials to become public. You can read this file and from it mine a great deal of information about the case.

For example, a search warrant might sound rather dull, but for the writer chasing a story it can be an exciting discovery. To get a search warrant from a judge, a police officer has to give the judge his reasons; that is, he has to reveal information which suggests that a specific item of evidence probably can be found at a specific address.

The true crime book that I am writing now, temporarily titled *Deadly Secrets*, features a defendant who, allegedly, videotaped a murder. In the court file I found a search warrant written by an officer requesting permission to search the defendant's house for the videotape. Here is just a small part of the officer's statement in the warrant. It concerns a different shooting, which led to the revelation about the videotaping of the earlier murder.

On Saturday, November 4, 1989, your affiant [the person testifying: here, the officer] responded to 2505 N. Halifax Drive in reference to a shooting. Upon your affiant's arrival he determined that a burglary had occurred and that the intruder had been shot dead by Konstantinos Fotopoulos. The intruder's body was discovered in an upstairs bedroom. Your affiant also determined that Lisa Fotopoulos had also been shot once in the head and had already been moved to the hospital for treatment. Your affiant also talked to Konstantinos Fotopoulos who advised that at approximately 4:50 A.M. he was awakened by a loud noise and saw a subject standing over his wife who was in bed next to him. Konstantinos Fotopoulos told your affiant that he took out a handgun from under the bed and fired several times, hitting the intruder.

There is much more, of course. This is just a sample to show you the sort of thing you might find, and the richness of detail that is in a document written by a police officer who was there when a crime was first being investigated.

Certainly the most valuable material you will find in a court file, and the bulk of the file, is the depositions. In a criminal case each potential witness must be deposed, that is, he must be questioned under oath by attorneys for the state or county, in the presence of his own lawyer. Also present are lawyers for the defendants in the case, and these lawyers also question the witness. Every word is taken down by a stenographer and eventually transcribed.

The result of all this is that the depositions become detailed interviews about the witness's knowledge of the crime. Most depositions contain very little personal information, though witnesses are asked their age and place of employment. Some depositions have a good deal of personal information. But all depositions are filled with information concerning the case, information which may never come out in the trial if the particular witness isn't called.

For *Deadly Secrets*, I have read depositions from dozens of police officers (describing their investigation), lab specialists (discussing ballistics, blood samples, carpet fibers found in the victim's clothing, etc.), people who were approached by the defendant (describing how he asked them to commit murder), relatives of one victim (describing his behavior before the shooting), relatives of the defendant (describing recent events in his life), etc.

Reading depositions can sometimes get tedious. There is a lot of repetition and there is a lot of testimony that you will never use. It is not unusual, for example, to find a 100- to 200-page deposition in which the medical examiner explains all his technical findings, material which may never get into your book. But keep in mind that if you read the depositions you may not have to cover the trial or even read the trial transcript. It is said among trial lawyers that you never ask a question unless you know what the answer is going to be. It is those depositions that give the lawyers the answers they are seeking. The depositions become a kind of rehearsal for the trial, and there may be nothing revealed in a trial that is not in the depositions. Also keep in mind that a witness is deposed relatively close to the events he is discussing, so his memory is much fresher than it will be at the trial a year or so later.

Of course, just because a witness says something in a deposition or at a trial doesn't make it true. Try to verify everything from another source.

Here are some sample pages from a deposition I have read recently for my book in progress.

1	WHEREUPON:
2	YVONNE LORI HENDERSON,
3	a witness, having first been duly sworn, was examined and testi-
4	fied as follows:
5	DIRECT EXAMINATION
6	BY MR. NILES:
7	Q. For the record, will you please state your full name?
8	A. Yvonne Lori Henderson
9	Q. How old a woman are you, Miss Henderson?
10	A. Twenty.
11	Q. I understand that you have entered a plea with the State
12	Attorney's office; is that correct?
13	A. Yes.

14   Q. And pursuant to that plea, which I was there when you
15 gave it, you agreed to testify truthfully?
16   A. Yes, sir.
17   Q. Can you do that no matter who it hurts?
18   A. Yes.
19   Q. I am going to ask you a line of questions, Miss Hender-
20 son. If I ask you something that you don't understand, just ask
21 me to clarify it or repeat it, okay? I don't intend to confuse you.
22 I want to ask you a few questions and get to the truth, if I
23 can, okay?
24   A. Okay.
25   Q. Now, Miss Henderson, you were a friend of Deidre
26 Hunt's and because of that got to know Kosta Fotopoulos and
27 all of these other people.
28   Is that the way it happened or did you know some of them
29 first?
30   A. No, I knew her first.
31   Q. You knew Dee Hunt first?
32   A. Yes.
33   Q. How did you happen to meet Dee Hunt in the first
34 place?
35   A. A roommate of mine brought her home, because she
36 didn't have a place to stay one night.
37   Q. Who was that roommate that you were living with?
38   A. Sheila Rainey.
39   Q. Where was that?
40   A. On Grandview.
41   Q. Was this an apartment that you had?
42   A. Yes.
43   Q. So Deidre came over to your house because she didn't
44 have any place to stay?
45   A. Right. She had met Sheila earlier that night.
46   Q. Where had she been staying before, if you know?
47   A. I don't know.
48   Q. Did you know anything about her at that time; where
49 she was from or anything about her?
50   A. We talked and I got to know her and that was about all.
51   Q. About how long ago was this, about when was it; do
52 you remember?
53   A. Early August.
54   Q. And do you know where Miss Rainey happened to meet

55	Miss Hunt?
56	A. I think at the Whitehall.
57	Q. At the lounge up in the Whitehall?
58	A. Yes.
59	Q. Was Sheila working there?
60	A. No.
61	Q. There just as a patron?
62	A. Right.
63	Q. And they ran into each other and became acquainted?
64	A. Yes.
65	Q. And then she asked her to come home because she
66	didn't have anyplace to stay?
67	A. Right.
68	Q. Did she start living there after that point?
69	A. Yes, she did.
70	Q. Were you working at that time, Lori?
71	A. No, not then.

How do you get the court file? Well, the specifics of the process can vary from state to state, and from county to county within a state. But basically you go to the courthouse where the case is to be tried. Go to the office of the court clerk. Give him or her the name of the defendant and the date of the arrest or indictment, whatever information you have. Ask for the case number, or case numbers if there are several defendants. Then go to the records room of the courthouse and ask for the file on that case.

You will not be allowed to leave the building, or even the room, with the file. You can read it there, usually at a small table that is provided for just this purpose, and take whatever notes you need, or very quietly read into a tape recorder. You can also ask for photocopies of documents, but too much of that can cut into your lunch budget. All the courthouses I've entered charge a dollar a page. So choose carefully. Don't waste money copying information you can get elsewhere. For example, don't pay for a copy of a witness's deposition, if that witness is willing to be interviewed by you. He can tell you what's in the deposition, or he might even give you his copy. On the other hand, if you find documents that are rich in information, like the search warrant I mentioned earlier, it is well worth a dollar a page. ("Well, Gary," you're saying, "why didn't you just interview the cop and he could have told you what was in the search warrant?" True.

But it happened that a judge's gag order was in effect at the time, preventing any policemen from talking to me about the case, which had not yet been tried.)

THE TRIAL TRANSCRIPT

At every trial there is a court stenographer merrily poking away at a mysterious machine that looks more like an adding machine than a typewriter and writes in shorthand symbols instead of letters.

The job of the court stenographer is to record every word that is spoken in open court. This becomes the trial transcript, the official public record of the trial.

After the trial has ended, the stenographer or his employee will get to work typing up the transcript into a form you and I can read. This is a long process and the seasons can change twice or thrice before the transcript is ready. The transcript for Anne Capute's trial, for example, came to about forty volumes, with each volume running 150 to 200 pages. (Anybody who thinks writing is not hard labor should try carrying those volumes up and down stairs a few times.)

The trial transcript becomes public record and is available to you at the courthouse, just as the court file is. If you read it you will know everything that occurred in court, except for visual things like legs being crossed, notes being passed, eyes being winked, and fists being shaken.

The court transcript, obviously, is an incredibly valuable resource. In fact, if defendants and witnesses all over town have been slamming doors in your face, the transcript is a necessity.

Unfortunately, not all transcripts are typed up and made available. The rules concerning transcripts vary from court to court, and you should call the clerk of the court you're interested in for specific details. But, generally speaking, a transcript will be typed and copies made if the judge orders it, or if there is an appeal of the case. On a death penalty case, there will always be a transcript, and usually with a murder case, one will be typed. A transcript for the trial of a juvenile will not be made public record.

If a transcript has not been typed for the trial you're writing about, you could make your own arrangements with the court stenographer. However, this is almost always a foolish thing to do because a transcript can easily cost more than a new Honda. Having a transcript typed usually will impoverish you to the tune of about three dollars a page, which means that a transcript like the one I used for *Fatal Dosage* would cost around $24,000.

When a transcript is available you will probably have to read it at the courthouse, because even at a dollar a page for a photocopy, you would have to give up some luxury, like eating. If you have plenty of other research material you won't have to read every word of the transcript. You'll know what you need, and where it is. Each volume of transcript has an index at the front, telling you that Huey's testimony begins on page 50, Duey's testimony on page 107, and so forth. If Huey, for example, gave you an interview or a copy of his deposition, you don't have to read his testimony in the transcript. (Also keep in mind my earlier point that the deposition was given much closer to the time of the crime, before Huey and his lawyer had time to sanitize Huey's court testimony.) Also the transcript contains a lot of material that you just don't need. The first seven volumes of the Capute transcript, for example, are just jury selection. Unless you need to know that one potential juror was scheduled for gall bladder surgery a week from Thursday, there's no need to wade through those volumes.

I know this must sound as tedious as geometry homework, but actually a court transcript can be as fascinating as some paperback mysteries. And though there are a lot of pages, there are not a lot of words on a page. As you can see from the sample pages of the *Without Mercy* transcript, which I've included, there's lots of white space and many short answers.

I have been lucky. With two of my books, lawyers for the defendants had extra copies of the transcript and lent them to me. So before you sit all day on a hard wooden chair in the records room of the courthouse ask around. Find out if a lawyer connected to the case is willing to lend you a copy of the transcript.

Later, when we discuss technique I'll show you how to work transcript material into your writing.

Here are some sample pages from Dee Casteel's trial transcript.

1	Q. Who drove?
2	A. I don't know.
3	Q. You saw the car when it pulled out, though?
4	A. Right, but I couldn't see who was driving.
5	Q. You said you knew there were three people in the car.
6	There was James Allen Bryant, right?
7	A. Right.
8	Q. Michael Irvine, right?

9   A. Right.

10   Q. And who was the third person in the car?

11   A. I didn't know.

12   Q. You now know, right?

13   A. Yes.

14   Q. Who was that?

15   MR. KERSHAW: Objection.

16   THE COURT: Sustained.

17   BY MR. NOVICK:

18   Q. As I understand your testimony on Mr. Koch's examina-
19   tion, when they left that restaurant you do not remember—you
20   do not know why and where they were going. Is that what you
21   told Mr. Koch?

22   A. I didn't say that.

23   Q. You did know where they were going, right?

24   A. I knew.

25   Q. The location?

26   A. Yes. I knew.

27   Q. They were going to your boss, Mr. Venecia's home,
28   correct?

29   A. Yes.

30   Q. Do I understand your testimony to Mr. Koch that you
31   don't know why they were going to Mr. Venecia's home, that
32   you did not know at that time?

33   Did I understand you correctly this morning, or did I
34   misunderstand you?

35   A. I don't recall Mr. Koch asking me that question this
36   morning.

37   Q. Isn't it a fact, Ms. Casteel, that you knew that Michael
38   Irvine had picked up James Allen Bryant along with the company
39   of a third person, a third man, and were driving to Art Venecia's
40   home to kill him? You knew that, right?

41   A. No. I did not know that.

42   Q. Would you look now at page 24, Counsel, Ms. Casteel,
43   of that same statement.

44   You were under oath when you swore to that statement
45   with Detective Richter, were you not?

46   A. Yes.

47   Q. The middle of the page.

48   Do you remember this question and this answer: "Was
49   it your understanding, and was there any doubt in your mind,

50 | where they were going when they left the restaurant?"
51 | "Answer: There was no doubt in my mind."
52 | "Question: Where were they going?"
53 | "Answer: To kill Art at 21900 S.W. 134 Avenue."
54 | Those are your answers to Detective Richter's ques-
55 | tions, are they not?
56 | A. Yes, they were.
57 | Q. And were you under oath when you gave those
58 | answers?
59 | A. Yes.
60 | Q. Were you not?
61 | A. Yes, sir.
62 | Q. The same oath that you are under here in court, correct?
63 | A. Yes, sir.
64 | Q. As to the answer to that question, was your memory
65 | better on April 19, 1984, less than a year after the murder of
66 | Arthur Venecia, or is it better now, four years later, as to that
67 | question, Ms. Casteel?
68 | A. It was better in 1984.

COVERING THE TRIAL

The good thing about going to a trial for a book is that you don't have to read the transcript later, and you certainly don't have to worry about paying for copies of it. To cover a trial you simply call the clerk of court, find out when a trial is scheduled, show up early so you can be sure of getting a seat, then take notes on what you see and let your tape recorder capture what is said.

The bad news is that if you're attending the trial, that means there is no verdict yet, and usually no certainty that a successful book can be written. It also means that in all likelihood you don't yet have a contract to write a book.

If a trial is going to take place in your area, and you have the time to cover it, then fine, go ahead. But if it's going to cost you money and valuable time to cover a trial, you're better off waiting until it is over.

Jack Olsen takes it a step further. "I absolutely will not touch a live case," he says, meaning a case that has not yet been tried, or one that is on appeal. "Getting involved in a case that's not settled is just asking for trouble."

GATHERING PERIPHERAL INFORMATION

There isn't a lot I can tell you about how to gather information that is not directly related to your crime. That's because, depending on your story, the additional information could be just about anything. The main point I want to make is that a true crime book, to succeed, must have depth and richness far beyond the simple facts of the case, and much of that richness finds its way into your manuscript because you were resourceful and creative in gathering additional information.

Here, for example, are just a few of the additional resources I used for *Across the Border*:

1. Much of my description of South Padre Island, where Mark Kilroy and his friends went for spring break, is drawn from information I got by writing to the South Padre Island Chamber of Commerce and asking for brochures. Also I got a book on Texas cities from the local library.

2. The descriptions of Brownsville and Matamoros I got by going there with a notebook. I also took a camera so I could later refresh my memory with the snapshots I took.

3. Much of chapter five, "The Religion" is drawn from books I read about Santeria.

4. Also, before I went to Mexico I videotaped news reports about the killings.

5. For my chapter on satanism I read a couple of books on the subject, and I sent for transcripts of the Oprah Winfrey and Geraldo Rivera shows on satanism. (Many of the talk and magazine shows sell transcripts. For information on where to write for a list of available transcripts, watch the credits roll at the end of the show.)

I could list dozens more, but yours might all be different. You might need, for example, to call the weather bureau in Omaha to find out if it was raining on the day that Deanna shoved a screwdriver into her mother's head at the Nebraska State Fair; or the Nebraska Tourist Board to find out just how big the fair is and how many hog farmers attend; or the Nebraska state police to find out if screwdriver murders are common in the state.

The point is don't just think about what your characters did. Think about the world they live in. What movies were playing at the time of the kidnapping? Was there a baseball strike that summer? How was the weather? What other crimes kept the police busy? Did someone with the same background as your criminal achieve fame and success while your guy was slashing throats in a pool room? We'll have examples later.

INTERVIEWS

By far your richest vein of information is the series of interviews you will conduct.

In chapter two we talked about some of the people you will want to interview — criminals, lawyers, victims, police, etc. There will be many more than that. Who you interview will depend on the specifics of your true crime story.

For *Fatal Dosage*, I interviewed nurses, and people who worked in Piscitelli's law office. For *Finder* I interviewed Marilyn Greene's kids, her ex-husband, people who had gone on searches with her. For *Across the Border*, I interviewed customs officers, experts on Santeria, and a local man who had found evidence of satanism. For *Without Mercy*, I interviewed an ex-girlfriend of one of the murderers, waitresses who had worked with Dee, the man who bought the house in which the murders had occurred. Those are just a few of the people I've interviewed for true crime books. One of the top attractions of writing true crime stories is that it leads you to the doors of many fascinating people.

I used to be amazed when I'd read nonfiction books and in the introduction the author would write something like, "I interviewed 125 people, and I'd like to thank them all." A hundred and twenty-five, I'd think. Impossible. But now I know that such numbers are not only possible, they are necessary. Relax. I'm not saying you have to interview over a hundred people. I am saying that you'll do a lot of interviews and they add up quickly. Not all interviews are major. An interview might be just two or three questions that you ask of some expert on bone fishing or hot air ballooning.

Of course, there's a great deal to be said about how you conduct an interview. Entire books have been written about interviewing, most notably, *The Craft of Interviewing*, by John Brady (Random House). If you intend to interview people, you should read Brady's book and others. But for now, here is a brief description of what you should do.

1. *Call the person you want to interview.* Tell her what you want to talk about, why, and how much time you will need. Make an appointment to see her, or to call her for a telephone interview.

2. *Make a list of the questions you want to ask.*

3. *When you interview, remember that honesty, flavored with charm, is the best policy.* Don't try to convince the accused ax murderer that you think she's a fine gal who's getting framed, if that's not true. You just have to let her know that you sincerely want to hear her side of the story. I've gotten along well with the subjects of all of my books by just shooting straight with them.

4. *Tape-record every interview.* Begin each interview with some sort of acknowledgment like, "You understand that I am taping this interview for use in my book *Fatal Deadliness?*"

This sort of thing is at least as important to your publisher's lawyers as, say, oxygen, and if you can't provide him with a record of an interview, you might have to perform painful surgery on your book. We'll talk more about your legal reading later.

You'll be doing a lot of interviews by phone. So go to your local Radio Shack where, for under twenty bucks, you can get a device that allows you to make high quality tape recordings of your phone calls. (There's also a little suction cup device that will do the job, for under five bucks, but it isn't as reliable and the quality of the recording is quite inferior.)

5. *Go for the emotions.* When you interview the pharmacist who inadvertently sold the poison, you don't have to ask him how he feels about filling prescriptions. But when you interview people who are involved with the criminals or victims, don't find out just what happened. Find out how they felt about it, and how they feel about it now.

6. *When you transcribe your tapes, type on one side of the paper only.* That way you can cut the interview up with scissors, and tape it back together so that it reveals information in the order you want.

One other thing. I don't always begin with a phone call. Many times when I want to interview somebody I begin with a letter. If the person I want to speak to is in jail I have to begin with a letter. Or if I think the idea of an interview is a touchy subject with someone who was close to the victim or to the criminal, I will send a letter first so he can think it over, rather than surprise him with a phone call which could make him wary and defensive. Here, for example, is the first letter I wrote to Lawrencia Bembenek, the woman who later escaped from prison.

September 25, 1989

Lawrencia Bembenek
Taycheedah Correctional Institution
N. 7139 Hwy. K.
Fondulac, Wisconsin 54935-9099

Dear Ms. Bembenek:

I did not see the "Inside Edition" which featured your story, but my wife did and she said, "This one's for you."

I am a writer of true stories and I seem to be specializing in stories about women who were somehow victimized by the establishment.

My first such book was Fatal Dosage, the story of nurse Anne Capute, who was accused of a mercy killing and was tried for first-degree murder. She was acquitted. Fatal Dosage was published by Bantam and later became the TV movie, "Fatal Judgment," starring Patty Duke.

Next I wrote Finder, the story of Marilyn Greene, a New York woman who finds missing people. Ms. Greene had to overcome years of sexism to succeed at her career. (The book was published by Crown in hardcover, and will be published in paperback by Pocket Books.)

In January Simon and Schuster will publish my new book, Without Mercy, the story of Dee Casteel, a former waitress, who is on death row in Florida.

I certainly didn't plan it this way, but somehow these are the stories that attract me. I find your story intriguing and I would like to discuss the possibility of writing it. However, I don't think there is much point in writing it unless you are supportive of my project. I can get by without the cooperation of some other people, but I don't think I'd care to write it without your cooperation. I realize that another book has already been written about your case, but I gather that it was done by a small publisher and has not been widely circulated. The book I have in mind would be published by a major publisher with wide national distribution, and plenty of publicity for your predicament.

Of course all of this is tentative right now. But at this point I'd like to know if you are open to the idea of me writing the book about you and your case. Would you give me the interview time I need with you? (Assuming, of course, that the prison gives me the necessary visiting privileges.) Also, would you ask your friends and relatives to give me the interview time I would need with them?

I realize that this whole idea probably makes you feel very vulnerable, and it is not a decision that is made easily. I don't know how the book will come out, but I can assure you that my other books have always worked out in the best interest of the women they were about.

I'm including a paperback copy of <u>Fatal Dosage</u>.

Thanks for considering this. I'm also including some literature about myself. I hope to hear from you soon.

Sincerely,

Gary Provost

So you've found a great story, you've written a proposal and gotten a contract, and you've gathered information. Congratulations. All you've got to do now is write the book. That's what the next three chapters are about.

5

PLOTTING

By the time you are ready to write your book you will already have an outline, the one you included with your proposal. (To refresh your memory on what an outline for a true crime might look like, go back to chapter three on writing the proposal.)

That outline, most likely, was based on units of information. In your outline you might have a chapter called "The Motive" in which you are going to show all the reasons why Ronnie McPhereson felt he had to kill the wormy little bookkeeper who worked on the third floor of the paper mill. Then you might have a chapter called "The Victim," in which you show us that the bookkeeper was leading a double life — wormy little bookkeeper by day, wild disco dancer by night. This might be followed in the outline by a chapter called "The Crime." This outline is what seemed to be a logical, orderly way to write your book at a time when you had minimal knowledge of the crime.

But now you've done months of research. You're ready to write, and you know a lot more than you did when you wrote the outline. It's time for plotting.

You might be surprised to see the word "plotting" in a book on how to write true crimes. After all, the story is the story. You can't plot the truth. But you can. Plotting is selection and sequence. You plot by choosing what to tell and when to tell it. Your outline was written before you had a deep understanding of the story. Now you must plot the book, and it will help if you will think of the plotting process as just a reworking and elaboration of that outline.

While plotting is partly an activity like outlining, that is, an overall plan of the book, it is also something you do along the way as you write. I will discuss it in both of those contexts.

CHOOSE WHAT TO TELL

If you simply write a chronology of what happened, including the dull with the diamonds, nobody will read your book. Before you tell the story, you must choose what to tell. I can't tell you what to choose because I don't know your story. But I can give you some tips that will make plotting seem a lot simpler to you.

When you first learn about a true crime, you don't really hear a story. All you're hearing is a bunch of information. Nobody wrote it. You must look at that whole body of information and discern what is story material from what is not. For example, there were four murderers in my *Without Mercy* case. They all lived the same twenty-four hour days before, during and after the crimes. Yet, I wrote mostly about Dee and Allen, and very little about Mike and Bill. My story sense told me that an alcoholic waitress who was "the nicest person you'd ever want to meet," was more interesting than the others. When I chose what to write about and what not to write about I was plotting.

TELL A STORY

When I plot I begin with an understanding that I am telling a story, not simply reporting events. Telling a story is different. It means that I want to reveal events in a way that makes the reading experience compelling.

For example, if I were reporting the events of *Deadly Secrets*, the book I am working on now, it would go something like this:
1. A woman gets married.
2. One night a burglar breaks in and shoots her in the head. Her husband shoots the burglar.
3. Later, when she is in the hospital, she learns that the burglar was really a hit man hired by her husband to kill her.
4. Then she finds out that her husband had a secret life, that he had a girlfriend, was involved in another murder, and was also involved in counterfeiting.

That's how the material might appear in the outline.

The problem with that as a story is that the dramatic high point, the moment when the wife is shot, comes early. After that, we learn quickly that she survives, and we find out about a lot of interesting things in the past.

Looking at that as a storyteller, I want to get the shooting near the end of the book. I want the reader to know that there is a plan to kill Lisa. I want the reader to worry about it, to wonder what will happen.

Then, when the wife survives I have an upbeat ending. So before the shooting I will show the husband getting pulled deeper and deeper into his secret life of adultery, counterfeiting and murder. Throughout the book we move closer and closer to the point where the wife is supposed to be murdered. That will keep the reader turning pages.

"But Gary, the reader will know Lisa survived even before he starts reading the book because he'll see her with you on the 'Oprah Winfrey Show' promoting the book."

This is true, but there is a suspension of logic within the reading process, and for our purposes the reader doesn't know Lisa survives, until I reveal that in the book.

So once you have the facts of a case, you must think hard and long, sometimes for months, for the best way to tell it. And the best way usually is the way that is most like a suspenseful novel.

Of course, some stories have a natural shape. With *Fatal Dosage* I didn't have to agonize much. The events in chronological order made for a good story. A woman is accused of a mercy killing. She is indicted. She is tried. She is acquitted.

With *Across the Border* I began with the event that first brought the story to public attention. Later I had to go back and recount the evolution of the drug gang/satanic cult. The creation of the gang would have come first chronologically, but it would not have been very compelling if the reader didn't first know that Mark Kilroy had been kidnapped by the gang.

LOOK FOR PLOT POINTS

Once I have the general shape of my story I look for plot points . . . those things that move the story forward . . . and I try to build chapters around them. I work with the word *but*. *But* is a good word because it means, we're not done yet, folks. *But* is the complication, the loose end, the cinder that is still glowing when we think the fire is out.

Here, in part, is how I used *but* to begin plotting *Rich Blood*, the story about a Miami woman accused of murdering her millionaire husband. This was part of the *Rich Blood* proposal which I showed you earlier.

Joyce is a poor secretary, *but* she meets a millionaire and marries him.

Now she's married to a millionaire, *but* the marriage goes sour.

Joyce wants to end the marriage, *but* she thinks she'll be left penniless.

She perhaps has a motive for murdering her husband, *but* so do other people.

After the murder, police suspect her, *but* she passes two polygraph exams.

She passes the exams, *but* the court rules that they will not be allowed.

Someone claims to have heard shots at 3:30 *but* the medical examiner confirms Joyce's story that Stanley died around 5:30. (The M.E. later reverses his decision, casting doubt on Joyce's version.)

And so forth. Just when the reader thinks he knows all the facts you say, "but . . . ."

Of course there are also important story events for which *but* won't work. They are the *and then*s. For example, in *Without Mercy* we have:

Allen asks Dee to talk to Mike,

and then Dee goes to Mike and he says he won't do it, but he has a friend who might,

and then Dee goes back to Allen and tells him,

and then Allen gives Dee the first half of the payment. Etc.

Once I've got all my *but*s, and *and then*s — my plot points — I expand each of them into a few paragraphs. A *but* usually, but not always, becomes the new outline of an individual chapter. Of course I never wrote the Joyce Cohen book, but I went through this process during the proposal stage. For example, I took the second *but* on my Joyce Cohen list ("but the marriage goes sour") and added to it all the related information that I was aware of. When I was done, that section of the outline looked like this:

The marriage grew cold. Joyce was young and vibrant. Her husband had been handsome and lively, but after his heart attack he was not quite so youthful. Joyce told friends that Stanley no longer looked as good, no longer dressed so nicely. Joyce tired of her husband and he tired of her. For the last two years of their marriage they had no sex. Joyce was in constant conflict with Stanley's two children by a previous marriage: Gary, the up-and-coming lawyer, and Gerri the well-known Miami television news anchorwoman. Joyce and Stanley fought. She wanted out of the marriage. "You can leave," he told her, "but you'll leave this marriage the way you came into it. Broke."

Joyce had a horror of ever being poor again. She confessed to friends that she was afraid that she would be left penniless, that the court would look at her newfound reputation for high living and give her nothing. She talked to Tanya Tucker about her concerns about money. She worried out loud that her stepchildren would inherit her husband's fortune and said that her son, Shawn, deserved to be the heir. She mentioned to some friends that it would be nice if someone would kill her husband.

Once I've got all my plot points elaborated to that degree, I start my first draft.

THINK GOALS

As you move along through the writing of your first draft, you will be faced with the same question that I am faced with: What should I write next?

Of course that is a complex question and the answer depends on your story, your style, your approach. But I can give you a very big, important tip.

Think goals.

Plots move forward because characters have goals. Each character that you write about, major or minor, is on the page because he wants something. He wants to murder his wife so he can marry his lover. He wants to catch a criminal. He wants to disappear. He might have a negative goal such as not to be killed, or not to be found guilty.

There are major goals in a true crime, such as the detective's goal of catching the criminal, or the criminal's goal of blowing up the feed and grain store. There are intermediate goals, such as the detective's goal of getting the case assigned to him, or the criminal's goal of acquiring dynamite. And there are minor goals, such as the detective's goal of finishing up another case so that he can get the feed and grain explosion case assigned to him, or the criminal's goal of stealing a car so he can drive to the dynamite store. The minor goals, as you can see, are not chosen at random; they are steps toward the major goals.

At any given point in your book you should be able to look at the page you are writing and say of each character, "What does he want?" If you don't know what he wants, then neither does the reader, and if the reader doesn't know what a character wants, he has no reason to care what happens next. Would you care what a baseball player does at the plate if you didn't know the goal was to get a hit?

So as you write, look at the character you are writing about. Once he gets what he wants, don't ask yourself "What did he do next?" He might have gone on to Roselle, New Jersey, for vacation, but that's not what you want to write about. Ask yourself, "What did he want next that would lead him closer to his ultimate goal?" and then "What did he do to get it?" That's what you should write about. But if much time went by between actions, ask yourself "Did another major character want something and take action to get it at this time?" If so, then perhaps it is time to change viewpoint for a while.

Remember, your characters in real life have thousands of goals every day. They want to get up. They want to eat breakfast. They want to watch "The Wonder Years." Every little thing we do is in response to a goal. But you are not writing a character's life; you are writing his story. So build your plot around the goals she has that are significant, important, specific and relevant to the true crime.

ASK THREE QUESTIONS

Now, given the fact that the people in your book had many goals connected with their story, how do you know which ones are worth writing about? Ultimately, you have to go with your own instinct, but there are three questions you can apply to each potential scene, and they will help you decide whether or not to write it.

Question number one: Is there opposition?

Opposition is the essential element in storytelling. It can also be called conflict. It means that as your character strives to reach his goal, something tries to thwart him. That something can be another person with an opposing goal:

In *Across the Border* there is a scene where Mark Kilroy is kidnapped. The kidnappers have the goal of subduing him. He struggles and leaps out of their truck because his goal is to avoid being kidnapped.

The opposition can be another person with the same goal. In *Deadly Secrets* I discuss the conflict between Kosta's wife and Kosta's girlfriend. There is conflict because the two women have the same goal: Kosta's love.

Opposition can also come from nonhuman forces, such as a financial disaster, a blizzard or an industrial accident.

Question number two: Is it interesting?

When I am writing a true crime if I come upon some information that is extremely interesting I will try to put it in the book, even if there is no conflict. Usually, however, I will not write it in the form of a scene, since scenes without conflict rarely work. For example, while researching *Without Mercy* I interviewed the people who bought the house in which Art Venecia was murdered. They told me that the house seemed to be haunted, and that they had brought in some relatives to exorcise it. All of this certainly had nothing to do with the case, but it was just plain interesting and I knew my readers would enjoy reading about it, so I put it in.

Question number three: Is it essential information?

If you have information which the reader must have in order to understand the story, then certainly you will put it in. The question is how much space will it take. Most of the information in your book can be reduced to one or two sentences.

For example: Allen and Dee discussed what to do with the body. They decided to bury it in the yard.

That tells you all you need to know, but because the discussion involved goals, opposition and character, I wrote a whole scene. If Allen alone had simply gone to the house and buried the body, I probably would have used one paragraph to tell the reader about it.

If your essential information is not innately dramatic, if it does not involve goals and opposition, then I would just say it in a sentence or two.

For example, at the end of chapter four in *Fatal Dosage* I need the reader to know who was given the information about the alleged mercy killing. That's essential information. But it simply involved a few phone calls, no great drama, no significant goals or opposition. So I wrote:

The information was spread in many directions. Dr. Hillier notified the medical examiner. The hospital's attorneys notified the District Attorney. And somebody notified the press.

6
WRITING IT

A book like this should really be called, *How to Write the True Crime if You Are Already Capable of Writing Another Kind of Book.*

In order to write a true crime book or anything else for publication you have to first learn to write. That is no easy trick. It takes years of study and practice to learn to write well enough for national publication. This chapter is specifically about writing the true crime. It is not a course in how to write.

So in this chapter when I write about Description, for example, or Characterization, I am only capsulizing what you will learn about those things in your broader education as a writer. If you learn about those things from any good source it will serve you well because the techniques for writing those things well don't change from one type of book to another. So look at this chapter not as the last word on anything, but as a true crime supplement to the general advice on those subjects that can be found in a variety of books and classrooms.

You'll have to find your own classrooms, but I can get you started on the books. Here are some that I recommend.

Make Your Words Work by Gary Provost (Writer's Digest Books)

Getting the Words Right: How to Revise, Edit and Rewrite by Theodore A. Rees Cheney (Writer's Digest Books)

Writing Creative Nonfiction by Theodore A. Rees Cheney (Writer's Digest Books)

On Writing Well by William Zinsser (Harper and Row)

How to Write a Damn Good Novel by James N. Frey (St. Martin's Press)

Writing Novels That Sell by Jack M. Bickham (Fireside)

"How come you're recommending two books on writing the novel, Gary? Don't you know that true crimes are nonfiction?"

Yes, but if you are going to write them well you will apply many of the techniques of a good novelist. And by the way, thanks for not embarrassing me by pointing out that I also recommended one of my own books.

One more point. Even though we discussed the proposal earlier, to keep things chronological, I did not discuss the writing techniques you will need to write the proposal. Obviously, they are the techniques you will need to write the rest of the book.

YOUR OVERALL APPROACH

Just as a man and woman can combine to make a child unlike any other in the world, a story and an author create a book that is different from any other. You will bring to your true crime book your creativity, your originality, your way of looking at things.

However, in a more general way we can divide the style of a true crime into two types: reportorial and novelistic.

The reportorial style is almost like a news report. It provides information, but it does it in a one-dimensional way, without tone or attitude, and usually without framing it in a scene.

Here is an example of the reportorial style from *Murder of Innocence* by Joel Kaplan, George Papajohn and Eric Zorn (Warner Books).

Her calls continued to Arizona—up to thirty in an hour on one memorable afternoon—and Steve Witt called his old high school friend and college roommate Lou Spivack for advice. Lou was an assistant county prosecutor in Arizona, and calls coming from Wisconsin were out of his jurisdiction. His first thought was that Steve should get an attorney and file a civil suit to stop the harassment, but neither of them could find a lawyer eager to take on a case that would be complicated and financially unrewarding. His second thought was that such calls were felonies under federal law, and he might have luck getting the FBI to investigate and help bring federal charges against Laurie.

So Steve called the FBI. He said he wanted to sit down and outline his problem for them in detail, but the person who took the information over the telephone was brusque and unenthusiastic. Not a big enough problem. Not enough evidence. Maybe if he had taped the conversations . . .

* * *

In the middle of April, a group of students at the Towers got together to watch a televised interview with cult leader/slayer Charles Manson. Half a dozen of them gathered afterward in suite 810, dimmed the lights and proceeded to tell their own eerie-but-true stories of murder and intrigue. The door was open and Laurie, who was rambling through the halls again, saw the crowd and asked if she could come in. No one objected, so she plopped herself down at a desk and sat quietly for a time, listening to the vivid and increasingly gory narratives. Then she spoke up. "I've got a story to tell," she said.

Here is an example of the novelistic style from *Serpentine* by Thomas Thompson.

"I was holding my breath through it all," said Felix, when he told Charles the extraordinary news. The prisoner sat numb on the visiting room bench, slowly shaking his head in disbelief. Almost twenty-five years old, he at last possessed what most men are given the moment they are born—a legal identity. Felix intruded on Charles's happiness. There were two strings attached. First: Charles would not be permitted to live within the city of Paris for a restricted period after release from prison, due to the several crimes he had committed there. Second: Charles would be liable for service in the French military, like all the sons of the country.

At that, Charles grimaced. He had no desire to spend two more years in another kind of prison. Felix suggested that he not worry. Everything was at least a year away. Charles must complete his prison sentence before any new bridges would be crossed. With emotion, Charles threw his arms around Felix. "I don't know what to say except 'thank you,' " he said, weeping. "I promise never to let you down, Felix. I feel my life is finally beginning."

The distinction between the journalistic approach and the novelistic is one of degrees, not absolutes. The two can mingle comfortably in a single paragraph. Nonetheless, a few useful generalizations can be made.

The journalist tells, and the novelist shows.

The journalist sweeps his camera across events; the novelist focuses in.

The journalist skips the details; the novelist uses the details to enhance his story.

The journalist tells where information is coming from; the novelist does not. (For example, a journalistic approach to the first two sentences of the second Thompson paragraph would be "Felix says that Charles grimaced then, and told him that he had no desire to spend two more years in another kind of prison.")

The journalist does not create a scene, that is, a particular place and time; the novelist does.

The journalist keeps distance between himself and the characters; the novelist gets inside characters and describes their emotions.

If you write your true crime book entirely in journalistic fashion chances are it will be boring, and it will lack the intimacy which the reader craves. If you write it entirely in novelistic fashion, you will have to exclude a lot of interesting information, which cannot be written smoothly into a scene. Also the story will feel too fictional, and you will lose the impact that comes from the reader's awareness that the story is true. Most good true crime stories are a combination of journalistic and novelistic styles. The trick is knowing when to use which. I have some thoughts on that, but they will be more digestible if I save them for the end of this chapter. For now, I want to end this section by giving an example of how the novelistic and journalistic styles merge. In this excerpt from chapter two of *Without Mercy* I first have a scene—Allen Bryant has taken Dee for a drive so he can ask her something—and after the scene there is my journalistic voice telling the reader how the scene fits in to the big picture, and also reminding her that what she is reading is true.

After they had passed the Cutler Ridge Denny's for a second time, the one where Dee had made that awful scene on New Year's Eve, Allen cleared his throat nervously, like a boy about to ask for a date.

"You know what someone told me once?" he asked.

"What's that?"

"It sounds crazy, but somebody said you know a guy who could take a contract."

"You mean murder somebody?"

"Yes, for money."

"Who said that?"

"I don't know," Allen said. "One of the waitresses. What's the difference who?"

"Must have been talking about Mike," Dee said.

"Mike?"

"Mike Irvine. A friend of mine. Whoever told you that must have meant Mike."

"Who is he?"

"Friend of Cass's. I met Mike when I was working at the Saga

Lounge. He works at the Amoco station up on Three Hundredth Street."

"So would he?" Allen asked.

"You mean actually kill somebody?"

"Sure. Would he really do it?"

"Not Mike, no. Mike's a teddy bear, a real sweetheart."

"So he's not a criminal?"

"No. I think he sells dope sometimes but he's gentle. He would never do anything violent. He's a real sweet guy."

"So it's not true?" Allen said. "He's not a hit man?"

"A hit man? Christ, no. Not Mike. He's a kidder. He always says to me, Dee, if you and Cass ever decide to split, don't bother with a lawyer. I'll take care of it for you cheaper."

"You mean he would kill Cass?"

"Yeah, but he's only joking about it."

"Damn," Allen said.

"Why? Are you really thinking about having somebody killed?"

"Forget it," Allen snapped. "Just forget it."

They drove in silence for a long time. Now Dee felt sad. She had let Allen down.

"No," she said. She sat up straighter in the car. "I can't imagine Mike Irvine killing anybody. I just can't picture it." She stared out at the pastel blocks, the stores, the shops, the fast-food joints that went whizzing by, and she sensed that Allen was asking her to do something that was really important to him.

"Just can't picture it," she said again, as if to convince herself. "But. . . ."

"But what?" Allen said.

"But he might know somebody who would."

So that's how it began. Dee Casteel and James Allen Bryant went for a ride on South Dixie Highway, and the plan to murder Art Venecia was born in the front seat of the Lincoln that Art had bought for Allen. Simple. But not understandable. And a year later when the murders were discovered, people all over south Dade county who had known Dee as a friend or a waitress or as the woman down the street with two sons and a daughter, people who thought of Dee as "the nicest person you could ever want to meet," would read about it in the *Miami Herald* and they would wonder what in Christ's name was going on in Dee's mind. Why didn't she just tell James Allen Bryant to go to hell? Why did she go along with it?

"Why Novelistic?"

First of all I want to make one thing clear. When I talk about using novelistic techniques in a true crime I am not talking about writing a novelization of a true crime. That's an entirely different dish of potatoes.

A novelization would occur when, let's say for example, Barry Manilow goes on a killing spree in a K-Mart in Duluth. Maybe he strangles a dozen people with a badminton net from the sporting goods department, and when he is tried for the murders his lawyer claims that Manilow was driven temporarily insane by the constant harassment of the voice on the P.A. system saying, "Attention K-Mart shoppers." Then you come along while the trial is still fresh in people's minds and you write a novel called *Fatal Barry*. It's about a guy named Barry McDonald who goes on a killing spree in a department store in Nashville. Your Barry bludgeons five people to death with a Raggedy Ann doll and when he is tried, his lawyer claims he was driven temporarily insane by the Muzak in the store. The publisher puts a face not unlike Barry Manilow's on the cover, along with a few musical notes, and people buy the book because they think it is based on the Manilow case. This is fiction. It has nothing to do with true crime books. The books I write and the books you will write are called true crimes because they are true.

Okay, now that we've got that cleared up, we can get to the question: Why use the techniques of a novelist in a true crime? The answer is because we are in the entertainment business, not the news business.

When a newspaper reporter writes a story it is because, supposedly, the public has a need to know. So he must write quickly, accurately, and without great detail. When you and I write true crime stories we are not writing for the reader who needs to find out what happened yesterday. We are writing for readers who want to escape, who want to be transported into another world, another place. We are writing for the same people who read novels. If they pay eighteen smackers for the hardcover or five bucks for the paperback they don't want "just the facts, ma'am." They want color, character, emotion. The true crime writer does, to varying degrees, wear the hat of a journalist, but primarily he is a storyteller, and his job is to tell the story in the most entertaining, interesting, exciting way he can. The techniques of the novelist help him to do that.

THE LEAD

The lead for any kind of story should be provocative, not necessarily informational. It's more important to make the reader care about something than know about something. Certainly, an established professional writer can sometimes seduce readers with a well-written leisurely lead, one that sets the scene or describes a character's background before anything actually happens. That's because editors and readers know from experience that a top writer will deliver a compelling story. The opening of *In Cold Blood* is a good example of this.

Here is another example of a leisurely lead, from *Small Sacrifices* by Ann Rule.

There is no more idyllic spot in May than the Willamette Valley that cradles Eugene and Springfield, Oregon. Sheltered by the Cascade Range to the east and the steel-blue and purple ridges of the coastal mountains on the western horizon, the valley was an oasis for pioneers more than a century ago. It remains an oasis today. Rivers thread their way through Eugene and Springfield: the Willamette, the McKenzie, the Mohawk, the Little Mohawk — nourishing the land.

However, that kind of lead is risky for the established writer and possibly fatal for the newcomer. When Ann Rule wrote *Small Sacrifices* she was a well-known true crime writer with a high degree of credibility, established mainly through the success of *The Stranger Beside Me*, her best-selling book about Ted Bundy. Her reputation was an implicit promise of a good read. But earlier, when she wrote *The Stranger Beside Me*, she did not have a vast audience of devoted readers. She had to write for millions of potential readers who had never heard of her, and many of them would stand in bookstores and drugstores judging her by the first page.

She began the way you should begin, not with scenery and history, but with a character in motion.

No one glanced at the young man who walked out of the Trailways Bus Station in Tallahassee, Florida, at dawn on Sunday, January 8, 1978. He looked like a college student — perhaps a bit older — and he blended in smoothly with the 30,000 students who had arrived in Florida's capital city that week. He had planned it that way. He felt at ease in a campus atmosphere, at home.

So don't open your book with a description of the town, or a sketchy biography of the main character. Do what most of the top writers do. Get the reader involved in a situation immediately. It doesn't have to be a murder in progress or a trial. It just has to be something that matters to the characters.

In my Writer's Retreat Workshop I often ask my students, "How many of you care what the weather is like in Duluth right now?" Nobody raises a hand. Then I ask, "How many would care if they had a sister or a husband flying into Duluth?"

The point is that your reader will care a lot more about the description of the town after he knows some of the people who live in the town.

Here is how Thomas Thompson began *Blood and Money*, one of the most successful true crime books ever.

During the night an early spring rain washed the city and now, at dawn, the air was sweet and heavy. Remnants of fog still held to the pavements of Houston, rolling across the streets like cobweb tumbleweeds, and the windshields of early commuters were misted and dangerous. The morning seemed sad, of little promise.

In his bed, the old man sweated and tossed. This night had been worse than most. He had awakened over and over again, and each time he checked the clock. He was impatient for the new day to commence so that he could order the flowers. One hundred perfect yellow roses would surely please his daughter. Not until he saw her laugh again would he sleep well.

After you've read those paragraphs you don't know who the old man is or where he was born, or what kind of furniture he has. You don't know where the daughter went to school or who she's married to or what kind of wine she favors. You don't know much of anything about either of them. You don't have answers. What you have is questions, and they are questions that you find interesting. Why did the morning seem sad? Why did the old man keep waking up during the night? Why was the daughter unable to laugh? How could the man afford to send a hundred yellow roses?

This is what a good lead does. It gets the reader asking questions, and the reader keeps turning pages to get answers to those questions. Your job as writer is to always create more questions than answers until you get to the last page.

A SENSE OF PLACE

In most true crimes the setting is almost a character in the story. It becomes often an influential force in the events. Whether it is the Kansas of *In Cold Blood*, the Texas of *Blood and Money*, or the south of *Bitter Blood*, the reader is left with the feeling that if all of the characters in the story were exported to another state or region, the story would not have happened, at least not in the same way. Editors, when asked the ingredients of a good true crime, almost always mention a sense of place.

In his preface to *Bad Blood: A Family Murder in Marin County*, Richard M. Levine talks about the significance of place in his true story:

"This is a story of parents and their children that takes place in Marin County," he writes. "Not the familiar Marin County of encounter sessions and hot tubs in eucalyptus groves, but one that exists farther up the freeway, where tract houses surrounded by high fences come in four standard colors." In various ways he implies that the crime he writes of — a teenaged boy and girl murder her parents — was nourished by the soil of that particular place and time.

Here is an example of how he creates a sense of place in the story.

Chuck and Marlene walked the remaining half mile from the mall to his house — past the Guide Dogs for the Blind training center, where Chuck had often played as a kid; past Reverend Walter Werronen's split-level Faith Lutheran Church, which his parents occasionally attended; past Hartzell Elementary School, which he had attended; across the railroad tracks to the Riley's modest three bedroom house in Rafael Meadows.

Technically a part of the city of San Rafael, Rafael Meadows was definitely "on the other side of the tracks" from upper-middle-class Terra Linda even if the trains, a freight-carrying branch of the southern Pacific, hardly ran anymore. The houses there were also tracts, but smaller and less expensive than Terra Linda's, while the residents more often than not held blue collar jobs in the area instead of commuting to more lucrative work in San Francisco. Although the Meadows was often described as "rundown" (or "lived in" depending on whom you were talking to) it had a neighborly, back-fence feeling that Terra Linda conspicuously lacked — a lifestyle perfectly suited to Oscar and Joanne Riley.

Notice how Levine doesn't just give you a grocery list of local features. He relates them to character. The training center "where Chuck often played as a kid," the church "which his parents occasionally attended," etc. all suggest a place interacting with people, not simply existing as a backdrop for their actions.

Keep in mind that a little of this place description goes a long way. Don't try to load every page with descriptions of houses, streets, mountains, etc. But as you write keep in mind the influence that place might exert on your characters.

CHOOSING THE VIEWPOINT

If you're a little iffy on just what viewpoint means in a story, read the viewpoint chapters in my book, *Make Your Words Work*, and Jack Bickham's *Writing Novels That Sell*.

Probably the most common viewpoint to be found in true crime books is that of the criminal. He, after all, knew about the crime before it happened, and he is often the only living person who was at the crime. He usually is the most interesting person in the book because he is the person who had motivation, and took action.

Perhaps the second most common viewpoint is that of an investigator, usually a police officer, but sometimes a reporter, lawyer or relative of the victim. The investigator is interesting because he is highly motivated, he is taking action, and because investigations are inherently interesting. You may recall that when I asked editors to name the ingredients of a good true crime every one of them included "an investigation."

You will also find books—*Perfect Victim* is an example—which are largely written from the viewpoint of the victim. These are less common, however, because the victim in a true crime is usually dead.

Few true crimes are written entirely in one viewpoint. In fact, I don't know of any. More likely the author will write some chapters or scenes from the victim's viewpoint—It was warm and sunny when Clarence arrived at work that morning. Things were looking great. He had just passed the one million dollar mark in life insurance sold. How could he imagine that within hours he would be crushed to death by a soft drink machine; many from the criminal's viewpoint—Katerina had always hated Clarence Moore, ever since that day in the third grade when he had tied her pigtails to a post. And now, with the Vic Bulk Body Building course completed, she finally had it in her power to get even; and from the investigator's viewpoint—Detective Ebert had seen this type of thing before, a soft drink machine toppling on a victim and made to look like an accident. Ebert was convinced that Clarence Moore had been murdered, and because the lab report said that traces of fresh nail polish had been found on the machine, he was convinced that the culprit was female.

In addition to these, and a variety of other viewpoints, the true crime will contain the author's viewpoint. The author as a viewpoint character is the reader's guide through the book, and he can do many jobs that cannot be done by other characters.

This is one of the big differences between a novel and a true crime written in novelistic style. Most novels are written entirely in the viewpoint of one or several characters. Virtually all true crimes, and that includes Capote's *In Cold Blood*, contain many passages that are in the author's viewpoint.

Here are a few of them, with examples from *Without Mercy*.

1. The author can explain things.

It is a difficult thing for the nonalcoholic mind to comprehend but under the influence of alcohol Dee Casteel was simply not the same person. She was somebody else, with different motives and different values. She walked differently, she talked differently, and everybody who knows her says that if you watch a "before and after" film you would not even be sure you were watching the same person.

2. The author can introduce documentation and evaluate it.

Only three people know exactly what happened to Art Venecia around midnight of June 18. Not surprisingly, their stories vary, and none of them in themselves are plausible explanations of what happened.

Here is how James Allen Bryant now describes the night: [This is followed by the statements given to the police by the three men involved in the crime.]

3. An author can speculate.

Why would a woman who is "the nicest person you'd ever want to meet" be skulking around in gas stations at three in the morning, working out a deal to murder a man she hardly knew?

There are three possible explanations. One is that Dee was so mesmerized by Allen and so afraid of losing her job that she would do anything to please him. Another is the compelling argument that the Dade county district attorney would eventually adopt, that greed was the motivation, that Dee planned to share with Allen in the proceeds from Art Venecia's death. And the third possibility is Dee Casteel's own equally persuasive argument: She never really believed there was going to be a murder until it was too late.

These are just a few of the jobs you as author can do by inserting your viewpoint into the book.

Okay, so now that we've got that covered, what about you. What viewpoints are you going to use?

I wish I knew what your book was about, then I could be more helpful. But I don't so I can't. All I can offer is a few tips.

The interesting people in any story are the ones who are highly motivated, and who take action. Victims are not inherently interesting. They are people to whom an interesting thing happened. Obviously if a major Hollywood actress is thrown from a bridge, it will make for a potentially more successful book than if a hairdresser is given the heave-ho. That's because it wasn't the murder that made the victim interesting. It's the fact that she's a big star. She makes the murder interesting, not the other way around.

So as you work your way through your book, gravitate toward the people who do things, not the ones who have things happen to them.

Also it will help immensely if you can find at least one sympathetic surviving character and write in her point of view part of the time. An investigator is usually a sympathetic character. Or you might write about the victim's wife or children. The reader likes to have somebody to root for.

Keep in mind that your choice of viewpoint will emerge from a combination of artistic and practical considerations. If Joe and Andy commit a crime and Joe won't give you an interview, but Andy is willing to yammer long into the night, then probably, as a practical matter, Andy will end up being a viewpoint character and Joe won't.

When I wrote *Without Mercy* I had four murderers. Three of them denied committing the crime. The other, Dee, did not. That's a practical reason why Dee became a viewpoint character. But also, Dee was much more interesting than the others because she was a woman, because everybody thought so highly of her, because she had kids, was an alcoholic, had a high I.Q.

When I wrote about the investigation of Venecia's murder I used detective John Parmenter as a viewpoint character. It was a practical decision because Parmenter's partner, who led the investigation, had dropped out of police work and did not care to be interviewed. But, as it turned out, Parmenter gave me a wonderful interview and he was the right person to use.

DESCRIPTION

Description is probably the most overrated aspect of writing by new writers. Most beginners write far too much description and they write it in a way that is isolated from the story. That is, they bring the story to a halt so that they can fill the reader in on certain visual details. They write something like this:

The city was dark and quiet. In the morning light the skyscrapers looked like immense spears slicing into the fog that hung somewhere between the sixtieth and seventieth story. A kind of dampness lingered in the air, as if the city had been washed at sunset, and now with the sun again rising over the East River, the air was giving up its moisture. The sound of taxi cabs skittering over loose and steamy manhole covers, rattled along the long city blocks. The stores, on the lowest level of huge brick buildings, were dark and still, their contents a collage of vague color on the greenish glass windows of early morn. On one corner a trash barrel lay on its side, and from it a trail of litter reached like a dying hand across the sidewalk.

This is static description. Nothing is happening, no character is being revealed, and the story is not moving forward.

Good description comes in short bursts. A sentence here. Two sentences there. And it is thoroughly folded into the movement of the story and the revelation of character. Good description does more than tell the reader what something looked like. It reveals the nature of people in the story. It keeps things moving.

Here is an example of description being well blended into story, from *Bad Dreams: A True Story of Sex, Money and Murder* by Anthony Haden-Guest (Ballantine).

When Melanie was young, New York was a city stuffed with delights. Her parents were living in Mayport, New Jersey, at the time, and she would be taken into Manhattan by her mother's aunt, her great-aunt Evelyn, a tall woman, thin to the point of gauntness, and given to conservative skirts and blouses, who had worked for the telephone company and lived in New York for thirty years. They would catch the train at Maplewood, rattle in on the Erie-Lackawanna line, and make a change at Hoboken, a dingy station. But Melanie was always aware of Manhattan lying ahead, its huge and glittery buildings pressing up energetically into the sky.

Description should be brief. Notice in the above excerpt that Haden-Guest uses one sentence to describe the aunt, one sentence to describe the train ride, and one sentence to describe the city. One sentence is usually enough to describe anything sufficiently.

Remember that description has no value of its own. It is only valuable to the extent that the reader cares about the thing being described.

CHARACTERIZATION

In fiction you create a character by what you invent about him.

In a true crime book you create a character by what you choose to tell from all the information you have about him.

Aside from that significant difference, characterization in fiction and in true crime is similar. You reveal character to the reader by the character's actions, his appearance, his words, and by speaking directly to the reader about the character. So make sure that the actions, descriptions, spoken words and whatever else that you choose to share with the reader are the ones that will characterize your real person as you see him or her.

Here is an example of how Linda Wolfe used actions to tell us something about William Douglas in *The Professor and the Prostitute* (Houghton Mifflin, 1986).

Forty years old and feeling that life had passed him by, Douglas packed up his briefcase, shut the door to his malodorous laboratory, and hurried through the empty, echoing corridors of the medical school. He would go to a bar, he decided. Maybe even get himself a prostitute. It wouldn't be the first time. And where was the harm, as long as Nancy and the children didn't know?

Here is Wolfe using description to tell us about the prostitute Robin Benedict, in the same book.

Robin Benedict must have been a lot like Sabrina. Certainly, she was beautiful, slim and willowy with wide dark eyes, luxuriant raven-colored hair, and smooth pale skin with an underglow of topaz and tourmaline. She dressed conservatively, wearing slacks or skirts with matching blazers. And she had a lively outgoing manner, a high-spirited way of putting shy men at ease.

Here is Jack Olsen, revealing character through the character's own spoken words in *Cold Kill* (Atheneum, 1988).

Sometimes he cut her short. One night he hung up. She called back and whined, "Oh David, what have I ever done to be treated like this?"

"Cindy," he said, "you haven't done anything. It's just that you keep running off at the mouth about mindless driveling bullshit, ya know?" He told her that she needed help and attention—but not his. "I already struck out, Cindy, I'm sorry."

And finally, from *The Mormon Murders* (Weidenfeld & Nicolson, 1988), here are Steven Naifeh and Gregory White Smith revealing character by speaking directly to the reader.

To her friends, she was the perfect Mormon. Generous, thoughtful, forgiving, community minded, she represented everything that was good and right about their unique religion. If only outsiders, who always seemed preoccupied with the Church's unusual doctrines, missionary zeal, and Victorian politics, could meet Kathy Sheets. Then they would understand the strength and appeal of the Mormon way of life.

She was certainly no ideologue. The *Book of Mormon* invariably put her to sleep.

QUOTES AND DIALOGUE

The words your characters speak are probably the most important words in your true crime book. Those words will be spoken either directly to the reader by your characters as you quote them, or in dialogue between two or more of your characters. These spoken words are the most important because they are a primary source for the story.

They are words spoken by participants, people who were there, lived the story.

Nobody can tell you exactly when to use spoken words and when to use your own, but here are some guidelines for quotes.

1. Quote characters when they have said something in a way that is more interesting than the way you might have said it, because the character was witty, or colorful, or somehow clever in what he said.

"We had money after we done it, that's for sure. We had enough money to burn a wet mule."

2. Quote people when what they are saying has emotional, not just informational, content.

"It's all so crazy, isn't it? The way we think. Or don't think. I mean, does all this have something to do with the terrible things I did? Could love have made the difference? Who knows?"

3. Quote people when they have been the active participant in some highly dramatic event, such as the killer describing the killing. (See the excerpt from *In Cold Blood* in the next chapter.)

4. As we discussed in the last chapter, quote people to reveal their character.

"Yeah, I could see that they was going to kill Teddy. I coulda maybe done something, but it wasn't worth me getting killed over. I ain't no hero. And if I'd a gone to the cops afterward, those guys would have got me for sure and it wouldn't have brought Teddy back, now would it?"

5. When you quote people in a true crime book you can quote just a few words (Sorrell says that the murder was "a routine event" for him and his sister). Or you can quote them at considerable length. In *Deadly Secrets* I may quote the entire confession of one murderer because it is very compelling material, and it could cover three or four pages in the book.

The significant difference between quotes and dialogue is that quotes don't have opposition. You, the author, are just saying that Joe said such and such either to you in an interview or to some other person. In dialogue there is opposition, there is tension. Joe says something, and then Harry says something that in some way opposes Joe, so Joe says something to oppose Harry, then Harry says something. Harry and Joe become like two boxers throwing punches. The quality of tension is not always high pitched and it is not always obvious, but it is always there.

In a little while we'll be discussing writing in scenes, and I will tell you that scenes contain tension. Usually the tension in a scene is reflected in the dialogue. If there is no tension in the dialogue don't write it. If there is no tension in the scene don't write it. Simply tell the reader what happened and use quotes, which don't require tension.

Here are a few more tips about dialogue in the true crime.

Dialogue should be short. That is, no speaker should go on too long without interruption. If your speaker goes on for more than a paragraph, the dialogue will sound like a sermon, or like your taped interview, but it will not sound like a conversation.

Don't waste dialogue on chit chat, like introductions:

"Merv this is Rhonda."

"Oh, hi, Rhonda, I'm Merv, this is my friend Sidney."

"Hi Sidney, nice to meet you. I'm Rhonda, and I'd like to introduce my sister Clarice."

Dialogue should reveal character or move the story forward, or both.

Incidentally, keep in mind that there's no law that says you have to use dialogue at all in your books. I use quite a bit of it, and that's why I'm talking about it. But many fine true crime writers don't use any dialogue. Every spoken word is delivered to the reader in the form of a quote.

Here is an example of dialogue in a true crime, a scene I wrote in *Fatal Dosage*.

Two nights later, Anne and Charlie went out to dinner with some friends in Hanover. On the drive home Anne told Charlie about the visit with Bonnie. Anne explained her realization that Bonnie and she lived now in two different worlds, that they had grown apart because they care about different things.

"It's not a case of one of us being right and one of us being wrong," Anne said. "It's just that we're different. We're not right for each other."

After a moment of silence Anne added, "Like you and me, Charlie."

Charlie didn't respond. Anne had made comments like that before. Charlie usually ignored them, and Anne usually didn't pursue them.

"I guess you know I'll be leaving you," Anne said. She was surprised that she had found the strength to say it.

Charlie twitched. "I can understand your saying that," Charlie said.

Anne was annoyed. Charlie sounded more like a therapist than a husband. "You can understand that I'm leaving you?" she said.

Charlie forced a smile. He stared straight ahead at the dark highway. "Well, no, not that," he said. "I mean, I can understand that you feel that way. You've been under so much pressure, you probably want to run away from everything."

"You got it," Anne said.

"But when all this is over—"

"When all this is over I'll either be in prison or Montana," Anne said. "Or California. Or someplace else, as long as it's far away from here."

"Why do you say that?" Charlie asked. He sounded hurt.

"Charlie, our marriage was over a long time ago. You know that. We just live together. We're roommates."

"We don't fight," he said.

"I know we don't fight. If we did, I'd be gone yesterday. We don't fight because we don't care enough about each other to fight." Anne smiled. Now she was the one who sounded like a therapist.

"Well, I've been pretty busy lately," Charlie said. "It's the feast season and all."

"Charlie, let's cut the bullshit, okay? We're not talking months here, we're talking years. And I'm not blaming you. It's not just you. It's us. We're both wonderful people, okay? We're just not wonderful for each other. I read books every night while you watch TV. I'm a flaming liberal. You voted for Reagan. We're different, that's all."

"Well, I watch TV because I'm tired," Charlie said. "I work hard all day."

"Oh, for God's sake," Anne said. "I'm not saying you're wrong and I'm right. I'm not saying that, Charlie. I'm saying you're you and I'm me. It's just time for me to move on. You should be glad. At least you won't be married to a convict. You won't be—" she paused and honed a cutting edge onto the final word—"embarrassed."

"What does that mean?" Charlie said.

"Oh, come on. You know you've buried your head in the sand over this whole thing. You're an ostrich, Charlie. You don't want to know about it, you don't want to deal with it."

A moment passed. Anne knew that Charlie was looking for something to defend himself with.

"I helped you get through nursing school," he said.

"I know you did," she said, "and I appreciate that more than you can imagine. But it's just . . . over."

They didn't speak again that night.

WRITE IN SCENES

It is a rough, but fair, generalization that when you are writing in scenes you are writing in a novelistic style, and when you are not writing in scenes, you are writing in a journalistic style. As I said earlier, most successful true crime books contain both types of writing.

A scene can be just a few paragraphs long, but it is usually a few pages long. It is a scene if it takes place at a specific time in a specific location. Imagine it as a box. The vertical lines represent place, the horizontal lines represent time. Your scene takes place inside that box. When you cross any line you have left the scene. You might go directly into another scene, or you might go into some general journalistic, summary-type writing that occurs in no particular place and time.

If you write, "Teddy was a tall, blond-haired bear of a man who always smiled, and was surprisingly soft-spoken for a man who had spent twenty years in a maximum security prison," then you are writing journalistically. Nothing is happening in time and place; you are just revealing general information.

If you write it this way, you are writing a scene:

Annette waited at the hotel for the hit man to arrive. When he did, she was surprised. She didn't know what she had expected, but certainly not this. He came in gently and offered his hand for her to shake. His name was Teddy and he was a tall, blond-haired bear of a man. He always smiled, it seemed.

"I hope this isn't a bad time to talk business," he said, "but I'm kind of anxious to get on with this murder so I can get home to my kids."

Annette couldn't believe how soft-spoken he was. She'd been told that he had spent twenty years in prison.

The true crime writer constantly weaves the novelistic and the journalistic together into a tapestry which, ideally, appears to have been done the only way possible. Certainly there are long scenes, several pages in a single place and time. And there are long segments of what might be called summary material, that never stop at a place and time. But also there is the digression within a scene. Melanie walks into the kitchen. She shows her son the gun she has purchased, the one they will use to murder the uncle who has been sponging off of them. We're in a scene, but at this point the author might digress journalistically for a paragraph to talk about how easy it is to buy a gun these days in that state. Then we re-enter the scene, with Melanie loading the gun.

Another common technique is what I call funneling. The author provides you with general, journalistic information and uses it to lead you into a novelistic scene. Here is an example of Capote doing it in *In Cold Blood.*

The sheriff's office is on the third floor of the Finney County courthouse, an ordinary stone-and-cement building standing in the center of an otherwise attractive tree-filled square. Nowadays, Garden City, which was once a rather raucous frontier town, is quite subdued. On the whole, the sheriff doesn't do much business, and his office, three sparsely furnished rooms, is ordinarily a quiet place, popular with courthouse idlers; Mrs. Edna Richardson, his hospitable secretary, usually has a pot of coffee going and plenty of time to "chew the fat." Or did, until, as she complained, "this Clutter thing came along," bringing with it "all these out-of-towners, all this newspaper fuss." The case, then commanding headlines as far east as Chicago, as far west as Denver, had indeed lured to Garden City, a considerable press corps.

On Monday, at midday, Dewey held a press conference in the sheriff's office. "I'll talk fact but not theories," he informed the assembled journalists. "Now, the big fact here, the thing to remember, is we're not dealing with one murder but four. And we don't know which of the four was the main target. The primary victim. It could have been Nancy or Kenyon, or either of the parents. Some people say, well, it must have been Mr. Clutter. Because his throat was cut; he was the most abused. But that's theory, not fact. It would help if we knew in what order the family died, but the coroner can't tell us that; he only knows the murders happened sometime between eleven p.m. Saturday and two a.m. Sunday." Then, responding to questions, he said no, neither of the women had been "sexually molested," and no, as far as was presently known, nothing had been stolen from the house, and yes, he did think it a "queer coincidence" that Mr. Clutter should have taken a forty-thousand dollar life insurance policy, with double indemnity, within eight hours of his death.

In the first paragraph Capote has written generally. You can spot the general words like "usually" and "ordinarily." In the second paragraph he has put his readers in a specific place, the sheriff's office, at a specific time, Monday, midday.

I've called this section "Write in Scenes" not because every word in your book should be in a scene; probably half of your book won't be. I'm emphasizing scenes because I think that's what new true crime writers neglect. They just start telling the story . . . this happened, then that happened . . . and it all lies flat on the page, because it hasn't been brought to life through the art of showing, not telling.

You, of course, will have to decide which parts of your books will be told journalistically and which parts will be shown novelistically. But I can offer a few guidelines.

1. *Write a scene when major decisions are made.* Don't write, "Jack and Jill met at a diner one day and decided to kill the boy who had pushed Jack down the hill." Take us into the diner, show us the characters, let us listen to the dialogue leading up to this important decision.

2. *Write a scene when there is conflict between characters.* Don't write, "Ferguson and Polaski never agreed on how to run the investigation, they were always fighting about it." Show us one fight so we can see their different approaches to the investigation.

3. *Write a scene when there is great emotion.* Don't write, "Police officer Hanratty went to the Haden's house and told them that Jennifer's body had been found." Write a scene that lets us see and feel the emotions of Hanratty, having to deliver this news, or the parents receiving it.

I want to emphasize this because I've noticed over the years that many of my students will write scenes leading up to a fight or perhaps a tragic moment, and then they skip over it and write something like, "Later, when things had calmed down." They omit the best scenes. I believe that new writers have a tendency to avoid confrontation and strong emotions, as most of us do in real life. In real life, do what you want, but in writing you must go for the heart. Don't avoid scenes just because they would make you uncomfortable in real life. Those are the most important ones.

4. *Write a scene at times of discovery.* When the body is found, or the killer is apprehended, or the detective suddenly realizes the significance of the clue, all of those exciting moments should be projected on the screen of the reader's mind. They should be shown, not told.

5. *Don't write a scene when there's no conflict, no emotion.* If you just want to tell us that the investigation progressed, or that there was a lot of press coverage, or whatever, then just tell us. Don't have a scene of someone reading the newspaper, unless he's going to have a strong emotion about what he's reading.

USING SOURCE MATERIAL

Using Newspaper Stories

In chapter four I talked about several of your most important sources of information. Now I'm going to talk about the ways in which that information might show up in your true crime. Keep in mind that I am only writing here about some of the sources I have found most useful. For your story there might be many other fountains of information.

News stories, as I mentioned earlier, almost always have mistakes in them. So don't depend on a news story for important facts in your story, unless you can verify those facts from another source.

However, you can safely use newspaper stories to enhance your main story. They are quite useful in filling out your book. As you search newspapers for stories about your case, look also for stories that somehow reflect on your main story, that echo its theme, set its scene, or somehow give it a context.

For example, when I was writing *Across the Border* I looked through many copies of the *Brownsville Herald* for stories about Mark Kilroy and the cult killings. Since I could already imagine the finished book, I knew some of the other things I would need. I knew, for example, that I would have to communicate the mood of spring break, so I clipped out several stories with that in mind. In the following excerpt I work from four different news stories. Each has been reduced to one or two sentences, but together they help me make a point.

Spring break was in full swing by this time on South Padre, and the common denominator, it seemed, was beer. In front of the Sailor-man's Pub someone stole a van carrying fifteen kegs of Budweiser. (The van and two of the kegs of beer were later recovered.) In another incident, three young men were fined for trying to steal three cases of Miller Lite twelve-ounce cans from the back of a beer truck. A Houston man was injured when he fell two stories from his condominium while trying to steal a keg of beer from an adjoining balcony. And the owners of the Palmetto Inn reported the theft of three kegs of Michelob Light and four cases of Lowenbrau from a walk-in cooler. So there was, as there always is when kids gather for spring break, a sense of mischief in the air. But if Mark and his friends thought about it at all, they must have thought there was nothing the least bit dangerous about partying on spring break.

Later in the book, after Mark has disappeared and his father has arrived in Brownsville to look for him, I use the technique again. This time I utilize several stories I have clipped, concerning crimes in the area.

Though Jim Kilroy must have wanted every resource, every man-hour dedicated to the search for Mark, a reading of the daily paper would have shown him that the police on both sides of the border had their normal ration of crime to deal with, and the Gateway Bridge seemed to be near a lot of it. During the two weeks following Mr. Kilroy's arrival in Brownsville, an eighteen-year-old UT student on her way from a nightclub back to the international bridge was gang-raped by four men. A Mexican truck driver was robbed and stabbed to death while waiting to pass through Mexican customs on the bridge. Dean Scott, another UT student, was beaten and robbed near the bridge by a Texas boy and a Mexican. And a night watchman at a Matamoros car wash died in a shootout with assailants ten blocks east of the bridge.

USING THE COURT FILE

The uses you will make of the court file are as varied as the documents in it. From the *Without Mercy* court file I learned more about Bill Rhodes, one of the murderers, from a letter that was sent to the judge by Bill's friend. I got photos of the victims, the murder house, and the digging up of the bodies. I got the statements that were given to the police by the suspects, and depositions given to the state attorney. And I got police reports of the investigation. Everything a police officer does on an investigation is carefully recorded in daily reports. Here is an example of how some of that material showed up in the book.

On Tuesday, April 17, Ken Meier, along with Detective Jerry Todd, met Anne Chepsiuk at a doughnut shop in Homestead. There, over coffee and jelly doughnuts, she told them about the confession that Dee had given in front of Jackie Ragan. Anne also gave the detectives two pictures of Art Venecia and one of Allen. She told them Art's address and said that the bodies were buried there.

Later that day the detectives and Anne picked up Jackie Ragan. Ragan led them to Dee Casteel's house in Homestead. The detectives drove by, noting the registration number on the red pickup truck that was parked in the driveway. Later they ran a check on the number and found that the vehicle was registered to Art Venecia.

Of course, you will interview police officers for your book. But their memories are never going to be as accurate or as detailed as what they wrote in their reports during the investigation.

USING TRIAL TRANSCRIPTS

In an author's note at the beginning of *Fatal Dosage* I wrote: "Courtroom interrogations are lengthy, tedious and repetitive. In order to wring what I hope is compelling dialogue from twenty-five volumes of court transcripts I have, of course, had to cut and compress. However, every word of courtroom dialogue in this book was spoken in the courtroom and all of the courtroom scenes are true representations of what was said and what it meant."

That should give you some idea of how to use trial transcripts.

The courtroom examination of a witness in a murder trial can run for many hours, sometimes two or three days. It can fill hundreds of pages of transcript. As a writer you need to find the crucial exchanges in all of that, the moments of excitement, tension, revelation.

William Goldman, the novelist and screenwriter, has said that he begins every scene "at the last possible moment." That's an attitude you should adopt when it comes to using courtroom testimony in your book. Witness examinations begin with dozens of inconsequential questions like, "What is your name?" "Where do you live?" and "What is your occupation?"

When you write you should skip all that, or summarize with something like, "The next witness was Julio Martinez, the plumber who claimed he had been working under the sink when Mrs. Mertz was bludgeoned to death."

As you approach the courtroom dialogue that you want to use, simply acknowledge the passing of time. From *Fatal Dosage*:

Later that day in the direct examination Pina asked Costello if she recalled any questions that Tom Bosanquet, the personnel director, had asked Anne.

"Yes," she said, "after Anne had said to me, 'I must have killed her,' Mr. Bosanquet asked her, 'Did you realize that you had killed her?' or 'Do you feel that you killed her?' And Anne's response was, 'Yes, I do.' "

Then you can summarize the testimony that occurs before your next important dialogue.

Pina moved on. He covered the interviews that Costello had done with eight other nurses, and the phone calls between Costello and Anne.

For Anne the worst moment of the day came at three o'clock.

"Mrs. Costello," Pina said, "based on your training and your experience as assistant administrator for nursing services at Morton Hospital, do you have an opinion as to whether or not safe nursing practices were used by defendant Anne Capute in her nursing care of Norma C. Leanues on May sixteenth and May seventeenth, 1980?"

"I have an opinion," Costello said.

"What is that opinion?"

Anne held her breath.

"My opinion is that safe nursing practices were not followed."

(Incidentally, in this last exchange you can see one reason why court examinations are so long. Here the district attorney asks the witness first if she has an opinion and then what that opinion is. This is typical. Each question has to be broken down into several parts, so that answers will not be ambiguous.)

If you know your case well you will recognize those courtroom exchanges that make for compelling reading just as they are, not because they necessarily meet the criteria of good dialogue, but because they reveal significant information. Those sections don't have to be rushed with summary or explanation. They are strong enough to stand on their own. Here's an example.

"Dr. Sturner," Pat said, "did the autopsy report anything about finding morphine in the body?"

"There is nothing mentioned about finding morphine, no."

"And the chemist's report indicates no morphine was found in the body?" Pat said.

"That's correct."

"Is it not a fact that the chemist's report does not support your conclusion that Mrs. Leanues died of acute morphine poisoning?"

"I'd say that's correct," Sturner said. "It does not support my opinion."

"Doctor, are you telling us that solely upon the autopsy and the chemist's report, you could conclude that Norma Leanues died of morphine poisoning?" Pat said, raising his voice to rattle the witness.

Sturner, whose conclusions were based largely on the medications records, seemed to back off on several points under Piscitelli's attack.

Keep in mind that I've given examples here only of using the transcript directly in your book's trial scenes. While most true crime stories will have a trial associated with them, many true crime books will not have trial scenes. In fact, *Fatal Dosage* is the only book of mine that does have trial scenes. Does that mean you don't need the transcript? No. The trial transcript's main value is as a mine of information, like the court file. And like the court file, the information you glean from the trial transcript can be used throughout the book.

USING INTERVIEWS

Interviews are the heart of the true crime book—or perhaps blood-stream would be a more appropriate metaphor—and the only way you can fully appreciate their importance is to read several true crime books, and with each paragraph ask yourself, "Where did the author get this information?" You'll see that in most cases the answer is, "from an interview."

Like the court file and the trial transcript, the interview material can enter the book directly or indirectly. When used directly, the transcript of an interview takes the form of a long or short quote. A short quote, let's say under four sentences, usually appears just the way it was said to you. However, with a long quote—several hundred words—that is rarely the case. The people you interview will ramble, they will repeat, they will volunteer information you don't care about, or information that you are giving to your reader from another interview. The people you interview don't always know what you're driving at, and even when they do they rarely use words in the concise and economical way that a writer must. So you guide your interviewee with a series of questions, and from his answers you cull the ones that you need in your book, and together they become a long quote.

Here, for example, are some of the questions I asked Kenny Baldwin, a fireman who was once called to the house of Art Venecia, the victim in *Without Mercy*.

Who do you work for? Who called the rescue squad? What was Art wearing? Did you talk to him? What did the cops do when they got there? Where was Allen? How did he look?

When I put all of Baldwin's answers together, leaving out the information that was redundant or irrelevant, it appeared in the book like this:

Earlier that evening Kenny Baldwin, a Princeton fireman assigned to the rescue squad, had responded to a call from a kid who worked for Art at the nursery.

"I went out," Baldwin recalls, "and Mr. Venecia was on the road waiting for us, all disturbed. He had red marks on his neck and he said this guy Allen had tried to kill him. He just had on a pair of shorts and tennis shoes. I said, 'Why did he do it?' and Venecia said, 'Well, he's been stealing money for years out of my restaurant.' I said, 'Where's Allen now?' and he said, 'He's locked himself in the house.' So I'm a fireman, we're not into breaking down doors when there's no fire, so I call the cops. The cops came and they talked to Allen through the door, and finally he let them in and he said he had taken a bunch of pills. He was crying. He had on a nice outfit, nice shirt, nice slacks, he was pretty sharp looking. We figured these guys were lovers. The cops had to talk baby talk to Allen to get him to tell what pills he had taken. 'Come on, Allen,' they teased, 'now tell us what pills you took,' and like that. Allen was real mad, real upset about the way things didn't turn out, and having all the cops and firemen around.

"The thing that struck me, though, was we're putting this guy Allen in the ambulance, and his lover, Venecia, the guy Allen had just tried to kill, was all worried about him. 'Why are you taking him to the hospital,' he says. 'Well, because he took a bunch of pills and we don't know what he took.' 'Where will you take him? Will he be okay?' He was really concerned about Allen."

Most of the information you gather during interviews will not show up directly like that. It will show up indirectly. That is you, the writer, will tell the information to the reader in reportorial style, or show it to the reader in novelistic style scenes. You do this because you are a writer, not a tape recorder. From all of your interviews about a person or event, you draw conclusions, generalizations, attitudes, and you try to write them in a way that is fast moving and interesting. However, quite often you leave hints for the reader, indications of where information came from, which gives the information credibility.

Let's use, for example, my description of Art Venecia in *Without Mercy*. Venecia did not have any close relationships, except Allen Bryant, the lover who arranged his murder. But Venecia was a member of the South Florida Theatre Organ Society, and many of its members knew him. From one of the organ society members I got a directory of all the members. I telephoned several of them and asked about Art. I called several members not just to get new information, but to get repetitious information so that I would know it was reliable. When I interview several people on the same subject I ask them many of the same questions. Each person has different perceptions and it's best not to trust an answer until you have heard it several times. I also talked to Art Venecia's two aging aunts in North Carolina.

In the excerpt below there are a few points where I specifically acknowledge the source of information about Art Venecia, either someone from the organ society, or the aunts. But the important thing for you to see is that *all* of the information in the excerpt came from those sources. That is the indirect use of interview material.

Though Art Venecia was a combustible substance in the presence of Allen Bryant, he was, in the presence of others, as cool and solid as pocket change. He was an excruciatingly private man, and besides Allen, probably nobody knew him well, except his friend Ralph Anderson, who died two years before Art was murdered. But those who knew Art at all have only nice things to say about him.

"God, he was really a nice fellow," says Robert Edward. "I never heard him say anything bad about anybody."

"You couldn't have met a finer gentleman," says Vivian Andre. "There wasn't anything he wouldn't do for you."

"He was a very nice guy," says Steve Fitzgerald. "Very personable, very intelligent."

And so forth.

All of these people were friends of Art's from the South Florida Theatre Organ Society, and though they are quick to tell you what an exemplary human being Art Venecia was, how helpful, intelligent, well mannered, and talented he was, they are also quick to add, "Of course, I didn't know him very well." The description of Art Venecia that emerges in almost every interview is "loner." He had, it seems, many acquaintances and they laughed at his jokes and happily sang along when he sat down to play the organ, but nobody loved him deeply enough or saw him often enough to take strong notice of the fact that, by the end of June 1983, Art Venecia wasn't around anymore.

Art's father, Arthur Venecia, Sr., had emigrated from Spain during the Spanish revolution. In the 1930s, Venecia Sr. established a rum distillery in Cuba. There he met his wife, Bessie, and they moved to St. Petersburg, where Venecia Sr. started another distillery. Arthur Jr. grew up in St. Petersburg. He was a quiet kid, and his great-aunts, with whom he spent several summers in North Carolina, remember him mostly for his music. Arthur, it seemed, was always blowing into a recorder, rapping on a drum, strumming a guitar, or tapping out a tune on some keyboard or other.

By the time he entered the University of Miami in Coral Gables, where he eventually acquired a degree in electrical engineering, Venecia was able to make a small living playing the piano in cocktail lounges and gay bars. He was, apparently, a more social creature then than he would be during the Allen Bryant years. He had his share of romances, and photos of his life then often show Venecia surrounded by friends. To some people he was an odd-looking character; one friend describes him as "Ichabod Crane–like" because of his thin body and obtrusive Adam's apple. But most of the people who knew Art describe him as an attractive man.

Art's homosexuality remained for the most part private. There was nothing limp-wristed about him, and nobody describes him as effeminate. He stayed in the closet for most people most of the time, and when he did trust an acquaintance enough to open the door and reveal his homosexuality, it almost always came as a surprise. His homosexuality, along with the fact that he didn't work in the engineering field for which he had been educated, became sources of conflict between Art and his mother, Bessie. Bessie, like many mothers, could not believe that a son of hers was gay, and she was inclined to show up unannounced at Art's door, with a marriageable female on her arm.

Know When to Shut Up. I said earlier that the people you interview don't usually speak in a way that makes for compelling reading. That's why you have to summarize, paraphrase, interpret and combine the words that are said to you. However, you must be on the lookout for those times when an interviewee says something that is far more readable than anything you can write, either because of what he says or how he says it. When a person is an eyewitness to, or a participant in dramatic events, and his words can also be taken as truth, they make for compelling reading without the interference of the writer.

Truman Capote certainly understood that when writing *In Cold Blood*. Capote was a master writer and he could certainly have written a great murder scene. Nonetheless, perhaps the most compelling section of the book comes when Capote steps aside and lets Perry Smith, one of the murderers, describe the murders. Here is a sample.

And we never used the lights again. Except the flashlight. Dick carried the flashlight when we went to tape Mr. Clutter and the boy. Just before I taped him, Mr. Clutter asked me — and these were his last words — wanted to know how his wife was, if she was all right, and I said she was fine, she was ready to go to sleep, and I told him it wasn't long till morning, and how in the morning somebody would find them, and then all of it, me and Dick, and all, would seem like something they dreamed. I wasn't kidding him. I didn't want to harm the man. I thought he was a very nice gentleman. Soft-spoken. I thought so right up to the moment I cut his throat.

USING PERIPHERAL INFORMATION

In chapter four I said that the successful true crime book must have a depth and a richness that goes beyond the facts of the case. The writer must look past the sources that are directly related to the crime, and find information that will add detail, color and context to his story. In that chapter I mentioned some additional sources that I used for *Across the Border*. Here are capsule examples of how they showed up in the book.

1. By writing to the South Padre Island Chamber of Commerce for brochures I was able to write this:

South Padre, famous for its surfing, its fishing, and its warm and sunny winters, is a natural magnet for Texas college students. "Texas Week" in March, when 300,000 young men and women inject about ten million dollars into the local economy, is the biggest week of the year for the restaurants and hotels in the area. Besides its beaches and the presence of the opposite sex in great bathing-suited numbers, South Padre Island is attractive to students because of its nearness to Mexico, where beer is plentiful and nobody asks for an ID.

2. By reading books about Santeria I was able to write this:

More significantly, especially in the context of the Constanzo case, santeros believe that through divination the priest cannot only see solutions, but can, with magic, effect them. Just as Christians use prayer in an attempt to intervene in the natural flow of events, santeros use a complex form of magic which is called sorcery by some and witchcraft or voodoo by others. The Spanish word is *brujeria*. For the sake of simplicity we will call it magic. Furthermore, and this accounts in part for the hold Constanzo had over his followers, the believers in this and other African religions don't think that the priest's powers are limited to white magic. Black magic is also possible. In other words, the priest can create a spell that will bring you good luck, but he can also do a spell that will kill you.

3. By sending for a transcript of an "Oprah Winfrey Show" I was able to write this:

Television viewers have also been told about satanic murders that may or may not have occurred.

When Oprah Winfrey did a show on "Satanic Worship" in 1988, one man stood up to say he was a follower of the Satanist Church in Chicago and that at the end of one ceremony, he and others ended up murdering someone.

"It wasn't anybody I knew," he said. "And I reported it. They were stabbed seven times. It was about '80, '81. And the ritual was a witch's Sabbath, and it got out of hand, and the high priest brought out these seven daggers and they impaled him in the form of a cross with the seven daggers."

8

CREATIVE LICENSE

The term, "creative license" implies that the artist, in order to realize his artistic vision, can take certain liberties with the truth. The idea of creative license has been generally accepted. The big question has always been, "How much?"

Oddly, the degree of creative license that is considered acceptable varies from medium to medium. A portraitist for example could remove a wart from his subject's face, add some intensity to the lips, even raise an eyebrow, all without raising an eyebrow.

Movies that are supposed to be true stories routinely include scenes that never occurred and characters who never lived. This practice usually troubles no one except the people who lived the story. However, when the movie involves historical information, hackles are often raised. The film *Mississippi Burning*, for example, inflamed a good many critics who claim the film showed the FBI in a pro-civil rights posture which it never had. More recently, a documentary, *Roger and Me*, caught hell because the director allegedly filmed mansions in one community and said on film that they were in another.

Television has been the greatest purveyor of so-called "faction," the mixing of fiction with fact. We see docudramas, we see syndicated tabloid shows that use actors to reenact crimes, and even some respectable so-called news shows on the networks have caught hell for reenacting news events. One season we even had a weekly drama series about Elvis Presley.

With the written word, alarms are set off much more easily than with film or television. Even the slightest trifling with the truth can create havoc. Books have been pulled out of circulation for containing factual errors that would pass unnoticed on television. True, the inspiration for such action is usually the fear of lawsuits, not the love of truth, but it does seem as though the author who plays fast and loose with the facts is regarded as a particularly low form of vermin even by the people who aren't being dragged into court.

The problem, I think, is that many people regard all narrative nonfiction as if it were journalism. It is not. A good deal of it, including the true crime, is entertainment. People don't buy my books or Ann Rule's or yours to find out what's going on in the world. They buy them to be entertained, to have a pleasurable reading experience.

In journalism, daily newspapers, *TIME*, *Newsweek*, and so forth, much of what is being printed is history in the making. Lies or fictionalizing can make very serious changes in the perceptions the public has about who should be elected, what bills should be passed, what countries should be feared. Sometimes nothing less than public policy is at stake if a journalist decides to muck around with the truth. When journalists make up stories they are fired, their Pulitzer Prizes are taken away, their employers are embarrassed. And well they should be. Because there is such an emphasis on exactitude the journalist is also warned not to invent even minor details, such as the color of someone's hair, his age, or the wording of an answer. This is all very noble, but the fact is that reporters make dozens of unintentional mistakes every day.

When we talk about true crimes and creative license we're not talking about making up stories. That would be as wrong for the true crime writer as it is for the journalist. We're talking, for the most part, about those details. One difference between a true crime writer and a daily reporter is that the true crime writer often has no access to the details, so he makes them up; the reporter often has brief access and a tight deadline, so he gets them wrong. The result, of course, is the same.

So in the matter of creative license your true crime story falls somewhere between a movie, which nobody takes seriously, and a newspaper story, which everybody takes seriously. Your true crime story is kind of a mixture of journalism and entertainment. You have promised the reader a good read, certainly. But you have also promised him the truth. The only way you can keep both promises is to take creative license, but know where to draw the line. Where is the line? Ultimately, you'll have to decide that for yourself. But I can tell you what I do and think and what a few other true crime writers have to say.

Sometimes when I'm driving along Interstate 495 I feel as if all the cars that I pass are driving too slowly, and all the cars that pass me are driving too fast. My speed is the right speed. I suspect that a lot of true crime writers feel the same way. All the writers who take more liberties than they do, are crossing the line. So before I get too much into my view of this subject and my practices, I want to acknowledge that I think there are true crime writers who go too far. But I also know there are probably writers who think I go too far.

The matter of visual details is always a touchy one for the writer of true crime. I don't want to present only what Linda Wolfe, a fine writer of true crime stories, calls "the bleak bones of research." I want to create a scene so explicit that the reader can step into it and get lost in the reading dream. But, again quoting Wolfe, "There are things nonfiction accounts can never tell us, for invariably some of the principals of a story will not cooperate, or they hide their true feelings, or they are simply not in the habit of probing their minds and motivations to the extent or with the depth, that a writer requires."

Furthermore, few interview subjects recall what color socks they were wearing on a given day or whether they sat on the left or right side of the table. So when I write I must continually make decisions about what is a fair creation of minor details and what violates the promise of truth. No two writers will draw the line in exactly the same place. But there are some generalizations that seem fair to me. When I tell you what a person was wearing I either know it to be true or I have dressed the person myself, based on a general knowledge of that person's style of dress. When I tell you what a person said I either know the exact words or have combined my knowledge of the content of the conversation with my knowledge of the person's speech patterns to create dialogue. When I tell you who sat where and who drank coffee and who had tea, I am giving you the exact truth or my best conclusion based on the facts that I do know.

As for dialogue, people almost never remember the exact words that were spoken in a conversation months ago, particularly when the conversation was not significant at the time. In those cases where someone does remember the exact words, or where the words have been recorded, such as in a deposition, I use the exact words. In all other cases I base dialogue on what I know was said and the person who said it.

I'll give you examples of all this in a minute. But first I want to tell you what some of the authors and editors I talked to had to say on this subject.

Brian DeFiore at Dell said, "I don't worry too much about where the line is between facts and invented detail, unless I see something where it's obvious the writer couldn't know, then I'm disturbed as a reader. Otherwise, the matter is between the writer and the lawyer."

Charlie Spicer at St. Martin's Press said, "I worry sometimes about where the line is, but frequently I leave it to the lawyers. You can invent a little bit with physical description, but you have to be careful to document everything factual because our lawyers query everything, and they don't want the writer just to say something is true. They want the documentation. In terms of setting a scene I don't care that much if a writer takes liberties, but in terms of something like dates I do care because it is important. Reconstructed dialogue usually doesn't bother me as long as it doesn't overstep the line into libel, as long as there is reasonable proof that a conversation like it did take place."

Ken Englade, the author, says, "By the time I begin to write I basically know my characters and from various sources I have picked up details about them. Maybe when I interview a policeman I'll ask, when you interrogated the woman what was she wearing, what were her mannerisms, etc. and I'll put together a bit of detail here and a bit there. Sometimes you can say well, this guy always wore blue jeans, so I can assume he wore blue jeans at this time. You can do things like that, as long as they are not misleading. If a guy wore blue jeans 98 percent of the time or always combed his hair in a certain way, then you can write it that way. You're trying to make these people as alive as possible and it doesn't really matter if he had on blue jeans or tan duck pants."

Englade's last sentence there sums it all up. You're trying to make these people come alive on the page, and that requires a great deal of detail that nobody really remembers. And the details we are talking about are the ones that don't really matter.

Jack Olsen says, "My books take two years to write because I don't invent any details. But I'm not saying it's wrong. If a woman always sits on the floor or the ground with her legs crossed, then I don't think a writer is going very far afield to write something like that in a scene. If a guy has a habit of running his hands through his hair, but all you have is a transcript of the trial, then at a crucial point in your trial scene you might have him run his hands through his hair. I don't do that, but I think it is absolutely fine to do that. In your research you develop certain characteristics and physical attributes of people and I suppose you would be justified in slipping one in now and then without knowing for sure that it happened. I probably should do it. I'm not a fanatic. You can't be a fanatic about every single letter of every single word."

Even though writers and editors will draw the line at a different place I think you can gather from these comments that there are some points about creative license in a true crime that everybody agrees on.

1. A true crime without a good deal of detail would be a boring book.

2. It's unrealistic to think that people are going to remember such details as exactly what they or others were wearing, eating or saying a year or two ago.

3. The only way to get that kind of detail into a book is to guess at it.

4. The writer should never alter or invent significant facts, facts that could change the course of the story.

5. What the writer does invent should be based on some general knowledge about a person or place.

6. The writer should never invent details when he knows the real details.

Okay, I realize I have gone on like a long-winded preacher on this, but that's because it is such an important issue. "What can I make up?" may be the most burning question that the would-be writer of true crimes has. Now, for examples.

What follows is the opening of chapter twelve of *Fatal Dosage*. It is a scene in which Anne first meets Pat Piscitelli, the lawyer who will defend her against murder charges. The comments in brackets are what I am adding for this book. They will show you where information is coming from. You will see what is invented and what is not, and you will also see that, comparatively speaking, very little is invented.

The drive from Anne's house in Plympton to Pat Piscitelli's office in Brockton takes about half an hour. [I noted the time when I drove it myself.] Anne drove it for the first time on January 20. She brought along her friend Beth Whitehead for no particular reason except that Anne didn't trust lawyers and felt better having a witness to the proceedings. [All true, from interviews with Anne.]

Piscitelli's law offices occupied all of a two-storied converted ranch house about a mile from downtown Brockton. While Anne and Beth waited in the lobby, sipping coffee, Piscitelli came out once to hand some papers to his secretary.

"He really is handsome, isn't he?" Beth said.

[I don't know if they drank coffee. I know that whenever I waited in that lobby I always drank coffee from the Mr. Coffee, and I also know that Anne is a coffee drinker. I don't know if Pat came out of his office just then. I do know that at some point in the visit Beth, out of Pat's earshot, commented on his looks.]

Anne grunted. "I suppose some people would say so," she said. "He's not my kind of handsome." [I don't know her exact words, but this is what she once said to me.]

Piscitelli, with his dark complexion, three-piece suit, and brushed back dark hair, was just a little too suave looking for Anne. "Rod Steiger is my kind of handsome."

[Piscitelli wore a three-piece suit every time I saw him. Anne's reaction is from interviews, and the Steiger remark is what Anne said to me.]

A few minutes later, when the two women were led into Pat's office and sat down facing his desk, the lawyer was equally distressed by Anne's looks. Her appearance would not be an asset in court, he thought. She was overweight, her hair was too short, and she was dressed too much like a man, in slacks and a plaid flannel shirt. She looks too tough to get a jury's sympathy, he thought. Some changes will have to be made.

[This is all true, based on interviews with Pat. It's also an example of someone remembering exactly what another person wore, because it was significant at the time.]

Pat introduced his assistant Don Harwood. Harwood had finished law school and was waiting to take the bar exam. He was twenty-three, good looking, well dressed. A future Piscitelli, Anne thought. She glanced at him, thought she saw a look of disapproval in his eyes, and decided that he also was not her type of guy. [All true, based on interviews with Anne and Harwood.]

Pat Piscitelli had already begun a Capute file. Now he sat behind his desk looking over the few papers in his folder. Anne fidgeted in her seat. She was uncomfortable with these lawyers in their suits. And besides, the last time she'd sat in an office facing a desk was when this whole mess started.

[Nobody told me that Pat looked at papers and Anne fidgeted. Those are my reasonable assumptions, based on Pat's routine and Anne's state of mind. The rest is from interviews with Anne.]

"Look," she blurted out, "there's two things I won't do. I won't plead guilty, and I won't lie to you." [That's an exact quote as Anne recalled it.]

Pat looked up. He smiled. [Reasonable assumption.]

She had broken the ice. "I'll accept those terms," he said. He pulled out his wallet, removed a dollar bill, and handed it to Beth Whitehead. "You're now an investigator for this office," he said. "That's your salary."

[All true, except Anne told me something like "Pat gave Beth a dollar." I made it visual by saying he pulled out his wallet, a reasonable assumption.]

Beth stared at him. [Reasonable assumption.]

"It protects the attorney-client privilege," he explained.

Anne watched as Beth tucked the dollar bill into her pocketbook. "I hope you work as cheaply as her," Anne said to Pat. "Before we go on, we might as well discuss money."

[Invented dialogue. I know that Anne was concerned about money and did bring it up. I also know that Anne was quick with a quip, and this comment is very much consistent with her character.]

Pat was pleased but unnerved. It was never easy to tell clients about legal costs, but it was necessary. He took a deep breath. [Reasonable assumption, based on interviews with Pat.]

"I'll need a twenty-thousand-dollar retainer," he said. "We'll worry about the rest later." [Exact quote, as recalled by Pat.]

Anne winced. "That much, huh?" [Reasonable assumption.]

Pat knew that most people could hardly imagine the reality of legal expenses for a case like this. "That's a drop in the bucket," he said. "I could use that up tomorrow by this time, just hiring expert witnesses. By the time this case is over you could conceivably run up legal bills of a quarter of a million dollars."

[Invented dialogue. I know that this was discussed then, and I know what words Pat used to discuss it later with me. As much as possible I created dialogue in which he uses the same words he used with me.]

"Well, that's a relief," Anne said. "Twenty thousand dollars I worry about. A quarter of a million dollars, that's too ridiculous to even think about." [True, Anne's memory of what she said.]

Now I'm going to jump ahead in the scene to show you a somewhat different use of creative license. As the scene continues Pat asks Anne to tell him her history.

She described her volunteer work at Jordan Hospital, and she told him about the school bus incident. Pat smiled when he heard about the citation and he made another note. He's keeping score, Anne thought. Points for me and points for them. Then she talked about her lifelong dream of being a nurse.

On the other side of the desk, Pat carefully studied Anne's demeanor, wondering how he would get the best out of her on a witness stand if it ever came to that. He saw that when Anne talked about her dream of being a nurse, her face softened. Her arms spread apart, she uncrossed her legs, and she seemed to glow. For a moment the music of her words transported him back to a dream of his own. He remembered a summer from his youth, spent in Onset, near Cape Cod. A woman had been strangled and dumped in a cranberry bog not far from where Pat worked as a pinboy in a bowling alley. The murder trial that followed was a sensation. It was the big story of the summer, and with a growing sense of excitement Pat followed it daily in the newspapers. Guilty or not guilty? What would the lawyers say? Would there be some new evidence? He was fascinated by the processes of law, and that summer of his thirteenth year he first dreamed of becoming a lawyer.

Now, as Anne talked about her dream of becoming a nurse, Pat found what he needed, a hook into the woman's soul. She had dreamed, and he had dreamed. And Pat knew from experience that the way to survive, to continue to care over the long and exhausting months of a murder case was to find in the client some part of himself. Anne was no longer just some tough looking gal who would have to grow her hair longer and put on a skirt. She was what he needed her to be, a street kid like himself.

First of all, that story about Pat as a kid in Onset is something that he told me when I asked about his ambition to become a lawyer. I knew that I wanted to use it somewhere in the book, because it was a good look into the man's character. Secondly, the insight that Pat had here about identifying with Anne occurred over a period of time. In real life these kinds of realizations rarely happen in a single moment. However, to make it dramatically pleasing I compress it into a single moment, and the catalyst I used to make it happen was Pat's memories about himself. I don't know if he recalled that Onset murder on this particular day. I do know that it represents a part of him that could interlock with a part of Anne and lead to the compatibility that did, in fact, exist. So here I have taken some general information which could exist in the character's mind at any time, and I have put it in his mind at the time when it is the most appropriate for the story.

So that's what I do and it is as far as I will go toward that line that we are not supposed to cross. What you do and how far you will go is between you and your conscience. You will find, however, that if you research thoroughly and conduct interviews with enthusiasm and curiosity, you won't have to invent much.

I have one more thing to tell you about this. It is a disheartening piece of news in one way, but it also will take some pressure off of you.

You'll recall that early in this book I talked about Truman Capote and *In Cold Blood*. I put him up to you as the father of the modern true crime. That is appropriate. *In Cold Blood* is a great book, and Capote was a great writer.

But he crossed the line. Gerald Clarke writes in *Capote*:

Truman did give way to a few small inventions and at least one major one, however, and *In Cold Blood* is the poorer for it. Following his usual custom, he had anguished over his ending, suffering so much from indecision that his writing hand froze and he was forced to compose on a typewriter. Should he end with the executions? he wondered. Or should he conclude with a happier scene? He chose the latter scenario. But since events had not provided him with a happy scene he was forced to make one up: a chance, springtime encounter of Alvin Dewey and Susan Kidwell, Nancy Clutters's best friend, in the tree-shaded Garden City cemetery, an oasis of green in that dry country.

Clarke notes that Capote's invented ending is almost a duplicate of the ending of Capote's fictional work, *The Grass Harp*.

Jack Olsen, by the way, is not quite as forgiving as Clarke on this matter. "Truman Capote," he says, "that little, gifted, brilliant son of a bitch put such pressure on all subsequent true crime writers, especially the ones who can't write as well as he, and that's all of them. He said that all of the quotes in *In Cold Blood* were verbatim, but we know he made a lot of them up. He sold the public on the idea of, oh, look folks, at last we have an accurate true crime book. He put such pressure on all the poor slobs that followed him to do the same thing, even though he hadn't done it himself. To me that is the single biggest outrage ever perpetrated under the name of true crime. If there was a gloomy setting in the courthouse, Capote wouldn't think twice about making it a gloomy day. *In Cold Blood* is a brilliant book, wonderfully written, and fraudulent."

9

TIPS

PHOTOS

"I hate true crime books that don't have photos," my brother Allan says. "I like to see what people look like."

Apparently a lot of true crime readers feel the same way, so most true crime books are published with photos, usually eight pages of them. The good news is that the photos will probably help to sell your book. The bad news is that most true crime book contracts require the author to supply the photos at his own expense. Consider yourself warned. This can get expensive. I spent over $3,000 to supply the publisher with sixteen pages of photos for *Across the Border*.

The best and cheapest way to get photos is, of course, to take them yourself. So get a 35 millimeter camera and learn how to take good black and white photos. Take photos of every person you interview and every scene that you visit. Take photos as early in your research as possible. That way if they don't come out, you have time to go back and take them again.

Another way to get photos is to ask the people you interview if they have photos of themselves or other people connected to the story. Of course a lot of the time, you end up with pictures of some kid who's got a telephone pole growing out of his head. Most amateurs take lousy photos.

And the third way to get photos is to buy the rights to photos that were taken before you got involved. This usually means getting copies of newspaper photos taken at the time of the arrests, or at the trial. You might have to cash in one of your CD's to take care of this little detail. To get photos from photographers at the *Brownsville Herald* I had to pay as much as three hundred dollars a photo. You could pay as little as fifty dollars, and once in a while a newspaper will give away the rights to a photo.

When you buy the rights to a newspaper photo you are buying rights either from the newspaper (or wire service) or the photographer.

If it's the newspaper, the price is probably set. With a photographer you can negotiate. Tell him that you are a struggling, underpaid, free-lance writer who doesn't have much money for photos. Also, point out to the photographer that it is a chance for him to have his photos in a nationally published book.

In any case, make it clear that you are buying the rights only to photos that are published in the book. Otherwise, you'll end up paying for photos your editor decides to trash. (For photos requested, but not used, you'll still have to pay a small processing fee, but not the big reprint fee.) Normally, you and your editor will discuss the kinds of photos that might go in the book and you will provide your editor with a large selection. She and the art director at the publishing house will choose the ones they want to publish. Depending on your publishing house, you might or might not be asked for your opinion. In either case, you will be given the privilege of paying for the photos.

RELEASES

As I noted earlier, when you tape an interview with a person you should begin with something like, "Do you acknowledge that I am taping this interview for use in my book *Fatal Poodle?*" That way you have a record of the person's cooperation.

However, the lawyers for your publishing house will sleep even more comfortably if you can obtain a signed written release. A release is just an agreement between you and the interview subject that says you are free to write about that person based on your interview with him or her. I've included a sample release. You can change it to suit your needs.

CONSENT AND RELEASE

FOR AND IN CONSIDERATION of the sum of One Dollar ($1.00) to me in hand paid simultaneously herewith by _____ of _____ (which together with its subsidiaries, affiliates, successors, licensees, assigns, directors, officers, representatives, agents and employees, is referred to herein after as "the Publisher") and for other valuable consideration, receipt of which is hereby acknowledged, I hereby grant to the Publisher the right to publish, in whole or in part, interviews given and to be given by me to representatives of the Publisher for use in, or as part of, or the basis of a [book] [article] (the

"Work") on [insert topic], with the unlimited right as the Publisher may in its sole discretion deem proper, to quote directly, to paraphrase, to edit, to rewrite, and otherwise to make use of such interviews; to describe and portray me under my name or such other name as the Publisher may elect, and to make such use of any episodes in my life, factually or fictionally, in the Work as the Publisher may in its sole discretion deem proper; to combine such interviews, description, portrayal and episodes with descriptions and portrayals of, interviews with, and episodes from, the lives of other persons; to do any or all of the foregoing in exercising and exploiting any and all further rights in the Work, including, but not limited to, such derivative versions of the Work as dramatic, motion picture and television productions based in whole or in part on the Work or such interviews (wherein I may be portrayed or impersonated by actors) and in advertising and publicizing the Work or such interviews and any derivative versions thereof.

I hereby agree that the Publisher may exercise all or any of the rights herein granted by me without claims, demands or causes of action—whether for violation of rights of privacy and/or publicity or infringement of any literary or other property right or otherwise—insofar as I am concerned. I represent that I am over twenty-one years of age.

Dated: _____

_____

Name

_____

Address

Witness

_____

Name

_____

Address

You can usually get by without a release for most interviews. After all, just the fact that someone is speaking to you at all strongly implies that you were planning to publish their words, you weren't just chatting to pass the time of day. But your publisher's lawyer may be edgy about a few people, and insist that you either get releases, cut material, or get the material elsewhere. The best way to protect yourself from this is to collect as many releases as you can get along the way, and present whatever you have to the publisher's lawyer at the legal reading.

You can probably get release forms from your publisher, or write your own based on the sample in this book.

If you are fortunate enough to sell movie rights to your book, you may find the producer's lawyers not quite so flexible. They usually insist on a release from at least one major figure in the story.

THE LEGAL READING

After your masterpiece is completed and delivered to the publisher, it will be submitted to a lawyer for a legal reading. The lawyer may be an employee of the publishing house, or an outside attorney. Either way, his job is to protect the publisher from lawsuits. Unfortunately, there are millions of morons out there who think that just seeing their name in print is a reason for them to be paid handsomely.

Publisher's lawyers do not have horns and a pitchfork, though it may sometimes seem as if they do. While the lawyer is trying to protect his client from lawsuits, he also understands that his client must publish interesting books to make money, and that the juicy revelations that could lead to a courthouse are often the same juicy revelations that can lead to the best-seller list. So the lawyer and you will cooperate to reach the same goal: A book which can make money that will not later be snatched away by a court.

The best thing you can do to minimize your own pain in a legal reading and to make life pleasant for the lawyer is to keep good records. Keep all your notes, tapes, newspaper clippings and other sources. The lawyer may not ask to see these, but he'll want to know whether or not you have them.

After the lawyer has finished reading your manuscript he will call or write to you with a series of questions. Most of them have to do with your sources of information. Was it printed in the paper? Is it public record? Is it definitely true? How many people said it? Do you have a release? etc. Tell him your source for each bit of information and he will tell you, "That's fine," "That's not good enough," or "Get another source." Some problems can be solved by the changing of a name, or the disguising of an identity. Others can only be solved by cuts in the manuscript.

My experience with legal readings is that they are never as harrowing as I expect, and I've never had to cut anything I was truly attached to. If you are careful and thorough in writing your book, you should not have many problems when it comes to the legal reading.

CHANGING NAMES

"A lot of true crime writers think it makes them look like extra good reporters if they can write that all the names in a book are real," says Jack Olsen. "To me it's an absolute guarantee that I'm not hearing the whole story. In the book I'm writing now, half the people will be under fictitious names."

If it's good enough for Jack Olsen it ought to be good enough for you. All of my books have some fictitious names. Almost all true crime books do. The fact is that some people won't talk to you unless you provide them with a different name in print.

"Take a guy I know who is serving time for rape," Olsen says. "He's got a wife and two kids. Nobody knows their dad is a rapist. Why should he reveal his name?"

While I agree with Olsen, I also think you should keep the number of fictitious names to a minimum. Readers, I suspect, are put off by them.

The important thing is that if you do change names, acknowledge it to the reader at the beginning of the book.

In most cases you will simply acknowledge the names that are fictitious, as I did in *Without Mercy*. Other times you might write a more general "Author's Note." Here, as an example, is what I wrote at the beginning of *Finder*.

We have tried to write a book that is honest as well as one that is sensitive to the confidentiality of client relationships. In most cases we have changed the names of clients and their families and, in many cases, minor details which might identify them. But everything else is true. The people in this book are real. The events we relate actually occurred.

M.G. and G.P.

LENGTH

The length of your book is something you will guess at when you make your proposal. I always say a book will be between 80,000 and 100,000 words. That's roughly 320 to 400 manuscript pages. That's the length I'm comfortable with, so that's what I write. Of course many true crimes, probably most, are much longer than that. Some should be. But even Jack Olsen, who has written books that long, thinks many are unnecessary.

"A lot of people seem to be buying books by the pound," Olsen says. "I like an eighty thousand word length. I'm turning in three hundred fifty thousand words sometimes and that's overexplaining everything, because I try to show everything rather than tell it, but I admire the concise ones."

For your first true crime it's probably best not to get too ambitious. Keep it under a hundred thousand words. Then if you discover that you have a story and a style that can support greater lengths, write longer books.

FIRST PERSON?

You might come upon a story that can be written in the first person from the point of view of the victim, the criminal or an investigator. Sometimes a story is much more compelling because it is being told by someone involved in the events of a crime. *Finder* is a good example. I started working on it in the third person, but later decided it would work best in the first person. After all, Marilyn Greene was the viewpoint character for every scene in the book, and she knew all of the information in the book.

On the other hand, a book like *Without Mercy* would never work in first person, for two reasons. One reason is that *Without Mercy* included a variety of information that no one person, except me, had. There was police procedural information I got from interviewing cops. There was alcoholism information I got from reading books. There was legal background I got from lawyers, etc. But the other reason, more significant, is that Dee, my main character, was a convicted murderer. Why should the reader believe her version of events? Any first person story in which the criminal is denying, or even playing down, his guilt, is automatically suspect.

But let's say you've found a story that could be told better in the first person than in the third person. Should you write it that way? You should if you can live with these realities:

1. You'll probably end up sharing money with the person who is telling the story.

2. Your name might not be on the cover. If it is on the cover it will be second to the teller of the story.

3. The teller of the story will be the person who is asked to appear on Phil Donahue, and do most of the publicity appearances.

4. People in publishing will know you wrote the book, but the general public won't have the foggiest idea of who you are.

On the positive side:

1. If you do a good job it could lead to other ghostwriting jobs, such as writing a celebrity's autobiography.

2. First person stories often sell a lot of books.

3. If you're shy and hate the spotlight, you won't be forced to appear on Phil Donahue or any other show.

4. A first person book is much easier to write, if the person you are interviewing can communicate well and is not a raving lunatic.

One final caution. Whether you are writing in the first person, or going into partnership with a principal for any other reason, get to know him first. I got along great with Marilyn Greene and Anne Capute. But I've ghostwritten other books with people who made me want to push a car off a cliff, with them inside it. Don't commit yourself to writing a book in cooperation with another person until that person understands that you are the writer, and you must have the last word on what goes into the book.

A CLIPPING FILE

"How do I look for a story?" says Ken Englade, author of *Cellar of Horror* and *Beyond Reason*, "I read newspapers. Friends send me ideas. And I keep a file of newspaper clippings. I have a special drawer and whenever I see something interesting I clip it out and put it in. Every month or so I cull through the clips. I ask myself, what is this story, what is the twist on it, does it have something special, something that attracts me. I'm particularly interested in the psychological aspects or legal point of view, so I could find stories that are good for someone else, but not for me. So it's good to be in touch with other true crime writers."

SHORT PIECES

There is a market for short true crime pieces, but it is not substantial and it does not pay well. While some big national magazines, like

Vanity Fair, do run true crime stories, your chances of selling one are not as good as your chances of selling a true crime book.

"The problem," according to John Brady, a national magazine consultant, "is that most of the national magazines that use true crime, use excerpts from new books or books in progress."

If you do want to write short true crime articles, keep in mind that everything I've said about finding a story, interviewing, research and writing technique applies. The market for these stories will be the dozen or so magazines listed in the "detective and crime" section of *Writer's Market*, Sunday newspaper supplements, and some regional magazines like *Texas Monthly* and *Yankee*. (Check your *Writer's Market*.)

If you would like to try to sell a true crime story to a magazine, approach them the same way you would for any article, with a good, solid query letter. Read the magazines you want to query, and read their market listings in *Writer's Market*. Some magazines don't want a story unless it involves great detective work. Others don't want cases that haven't gone to trial yet. The Sunday supplements, of course, want stories with a local angle.

For more information about query letters and magazine writing, read *Handbook of Magazine Article Writing* (Writer's Digest Books).

In any case, you're not going to get rich writing for these markets. Because true crime stories require so much more than most articles in the way of fact checking and multiple interviews, it is difficult to write a story that is both good and cost effective. The time you spend working on a true crime magazine piece, might be better spent writing a true crime book proposal.

10

SELLING YOUR BOOK
TO THE MOVIES

Three of my true crime books have been optioned for films, and a fourth came close. None of my other books have even been considered. (Though admittedly it would be difficult to make a major motion picture called *Make Every Word Count*.) A novelist could easily go through his whole career without ever having a book optioned for a film, so that .750 batting average for the true crime books is extraordinary.

There is a great deal of movie interest in true crime stories. After romance, crime is probably the number one subject in film. There have been many theatrical films made of true crime books, like *In Cold Blood*, *The Boston Strangler* and *Reversal of Fortune*. But the major market for true crime books that are turned into movies is television. Hardly a fortnight goes by without some true crime story arriving on the small screen. During a recent television season we saw the film versions of best-selling true crime books: Ann Rule's *Small Sacrifices* and Joe McGinniss's *Blind Faith*, but there were many more films of lesser known true crime books.

These books, like most film properties, are bought in two steps. First there is the option. That is, a producer, who thinks he can get financing to make your book into a film, buys the exclusive right to purchase it for a certain price within a period of time, let's say a year.

The second step comes when the producer makes a deal with a TV network or a movie studio to film the movie. If that happens then the producer "picks up" the option, that is he pays you the amount of money you had agreed to.

If the producer cannot get financing for the movie before the option period ends, then his option expires and you are free to sell the property all over again. Some properties are optioned many times before they are made. Ninety percent of the properties that get optioned for theatrical films never get made. Thirty percent of the ones optioned for television films do get made.

So, how can you get in on this? Well the first step of course is to write a proposal for a true crime book and sell it. At that point your project has credibility with producers. It's not just the idea of some would-be screenwriter in Podunk; it's a book that will be published by a real publisher.

If you have a literary agent, the next step is for him to send a copy of your proposal, or completed manuscript, to his affiliate west coast agent, who will try to market movie rights to your books. Some literary agents are set up to do this themselves.

If you don't have a literary agent, you will need to acquire a west coast agent to handle film rights. Getting your book to producers without an agent is very difficult. You will find a comprehensive list of movie agents in *The Complete Book of Scriptwriting* by J. Michael Straczynski (Writer's Digest Books).

Also, you can get a list of movie agents from the Writer's Guild of America, 8955 Beverly Boulevard, Los Angeles, CA 90048. There is a small charge, so you might want to call first (213-550-1000).

Approach a movie agent just as you would a literary agent. Write a letter. Tell him who you are, what you've written, who will publish it and when, and why you think it could make an exciting film. If an agent asks to see the material, send it along, to one agent at a time.

The movie agent will submit your material to producers just the way the literary agents submitted it to editors. However, there's one big difference. Editors read, producers don't. For producers, the idea needs to be boiled down. This is where you can help yourself immensely.

The terms Synopsis, Outline and Treatment are all used to describe various written forms of potential movie material before it has grown up to become a script. But the terms are a bit slippery. What one agent might call a synopsis, someone else might refer to as an outline or even a treatment.

In his book, Straczynski says that a film synopsis is a summing up of your idea as briefly as possible, usually about a paragraph. (In fact, your agent will supply producers with this.) He says that an outline can be anywhere from four to ten pages and adds, "There is some disagreement about its complexity." His advice is to write your outline in narrative style without any reference to camera angles and the like.

A treatment, according to Straczynski, runs between fifteen and forty-five pages and describes each scene that will appear in the screenplay.

Your goal, as the author of a true crime book that has been published or is scheduled to be published, is to get a producer excited with your description of the film. That description must be *short* and *visual*. You can call it a synopsis, as I did with the following example, or you can call it an outline. Whatever it is, send it to your agent and have him circulate it with the other material.

Here is what I wrote for *Without Mercy*. As you can see, it was still called *Delirium* at the time. This is a common way to present potential movie material, but it is not the only way. There is no one right way to do it. If you write something and a producer gets excited and buys an option, then you did it the right way. *Without Mercy* has been optioned but has not yet been made.

Gary Provost
% Todd Harris
Triad Artists

DELIRIUM
A film synopsis
By Gary Provost

Based on the book

DELIRIUM
A True Story of Murder Under the Influence
By Gary Provost

We see SUSAN, a young woman, park her car in front of the BROWARD COUNTY CORRECTIONAL INSTITUTION FOR WOMEN. Palm trees, etc. show us that we are in Florida. Susan walks across the parking lot, checks in at the front desk. They seem to know her. She walks through one steel security door, then another. She walks into a visitor's room. We see DEE CASTEEL. She is fortyish, attractive, but obviously beaten down by a difficult life. The two women hug. They are mother and daughter. They talk small talk. Dee asks about the boys. They're fine, Susan says. And then Susan tells her mother, "The state attorney wants me to testify against you." We see that Susan doesn't want to testify, she says she will run away instead. She blames other people for the mess she and Dee are in. Dee stops her. Dee tells her, "No. I'm responsible. I can't blame anybody else. It was my fault right from the beginning," and she stares off into space and we see the beginning of her story in flashback.

135

We see a family restaurant. Dee is working as a waitress. As she works her tables we see that she is a good waitress—competent, friendly, thoughtful. We also see that she sneaks alcohol into her coffee when no one is looking. She is an alcoholic. Through the restaurant window we see a blue Lincoln pull up.

ALLEN BRYANT comes into the restaurant. He is 25-30, good looking, very well dressed, and somewhat effeminate. He is charming, yet cold. Allen is the manager and he starts pulling money out of the register. Dee clearly seeks his approval. "Yes, Allen," "Would you like a cup of coffee Allen?" etc. Allen talks about Art, his lover. Art is driving him nuts, he says. Allen would like to get out of the relationship. Allen discovers Dee's supply of alcohol, and he bawls her out severely for drinking on the job. Allen leaves. Dee is devastated by the upbraiding. Clearly, Allen has an emotional hold on her.

At the end of the shift Dee is picked up by her daughter, Susan. Susan is a mature teenager, living on her own. In the car they talk about Dee's getting caught. We see that there is love and hate in this relationship, a lot of friction. "Ma, how could you get caught?" etc. Dee talks about her fears of being fired. "What will I do, there's no place left for me to go," etc. The daughter becomes the parent to the mother, "Oh, Ma, it will be okay." They stop someplace for ice cream. Now they are like two sisters and Susan tells Dee about the new job and the new boyfriend. We learn that Susan has left home because she hates her stepfather, Cass, who is abusive to Dee.

The following afternoon, Dee's day off, we see Dee at home with her two sons TODD and WYATT, active, good-humored boys, aged 12 and 14. The kids are happy because Dee has given up drinking again. The phone rings. It's Allen. He wants Dee to come to the restaurant later to talk. We see Dee washing and ironing her waitress uniforms. Clearly she expects to be fired. We see Dee take a drink before she leaves the house.

At the restaurant Allen is smiling. He asks Dee to go for a ride with him. During the ride he tells Dee he wants her to ask her friend Mike to commit a murder for him. Allen wants his lover, Art Venecia, killed. Dee says sure, fine, I'll ask Mike. She treats it as if it were not for real.

Dee tells Susan about Allen's request. Susan is angry with Dee for even getting involved, but she also deals with it as being unreal. Again we see the pattern of fighting and then making up between mother and daughter.

We see Dee in a gas station late at night with MIKE. Mike is 35-50, a hayseed, a good old boy who fixes cars and pumps gas. Mike agrees to do the murder, but in the banter between Mike and Dee we (and Dee) are never quite sure if he is serious or if he just plans to rip off Allen.

We see Dee and Allen in the restaurant. She tells him Mike has agreed. Allen is pleased with Dee and she is beaming.

We see Dee at home with the boys and CASS, her husband. Cass is 40-50, big. He's been drinking. There is a fight between Cass and Dee because Susan is coming for dinner. Dee taunts Cass, Cass hits her. Dinner is ruined. When Susan comes mother and daughter talk privately. We learn that alcoholism is the source of conflict between mother and daughter. Dee tells Susan about the conversation with Mike. Susan gets edgy, but Dee assures her that no murder will really take place, that it's all just talk.

We see Dee and Allen at the restaurant. They are both nervous. It is the night that the "murder" is scheduled. Mike shows up. Allen goes in a car with Mike and Mike's friend, BILL, who is 35-50, dangerous looking.

We see Dee alone, still at the restaurant, drinking coffee laced with vodka. We see the clock. We see Dee getting more edgy with each passing minute. On her face we see her realization that a murder really will take place. Dee calls Susan from the restaurant, tells her what's going on. Susan says call the police. Dee says I can't, I don't know where Art lives, besides what am I going to tell them, that I arranged a murder? We see Dee put down the phone, helpless.

We see darkness. As our eyes adjust to the darkness we see the outlines of a small, isolated house on a large piece of property. A car pulls up the long driveway, parks quietly. We hear the whispers of men getting out of the car, the soft closing of the doors. For a moment there is silence. Then we hear the voice of a frightened man in the house saying, "Take anything you want, only please don't hurt me." More silence, then we hear a chilling scream.

We see Dee wake up suddenly. It is morning. Her fears come back to her. She rushes out to grab the newspaper, thinking that if there was a murder it would be there. Nothing. She gets ready for work. She moves slowly, she is avoiding finding out the truth. At the restaurant Allen is waiting. They did it, he says, they slit Art's throat. Allen tells her she must help him dispose of the body.

We see Allen and Dee pull up to the house. Next to the house there is a trailer.

Inside the Venecia house we see Allen and Dee. There is blood on the walls. The body is in the bedroom. As they discuss what to do with it Dee becomes hysterical. Allen tells her he needs her more than ever now. She pulls herself together. She will be strong. They'll get rid of the body, put this behind them. Allen says "We have to tell Art's mother that he's gone away for a while." Dee asks, "Where does she live?" Allen says, "Right here. In the trailer."

We see Dee standing at the door to an old trailer in Venecia's yard. We see BESSIE, an old woman, white-haired, somewhat senile. She walks with a cane. She is Art's mother. Dee explains that she will be bringing Bessie's meals while Art is "away on business in North Carolina."

We see Dee and Allen moving the heavy wardrobe containing Art's body. They put it on a forklift, it falls off, they put it back, take it to the barn at the front of the property.

We see Allen cutting Bessie's phone line, and dead bolting the door to the house.

We see Allen talking to the employees of the restaurant, telling them Art has gone away and Dee will be in charge.

We see employees whispering, spreading rumors about Art being murdered.

We see Dee bringing meals to Bessie every day, checking out the barn where the body has been hidden.

We see Allen on the phone, pretending to be Art, liquidating stock.

We see Allen pressing Dee for Bessie's murder. "Sooner or later she will find out about Art," he says, "and then we'll all fry." We see Dee resisting.

We see Dee arriving at the house to deliver Bessie's supper. Something is on the road. It is Bessie. She has fallen while walking out to get the mail and has been unable to get up all day. We see Dee's concern.

Again we see Allen pressing Dee to go along with the murder of Bessie. He convinces her that it is really a mercy killing because of Bessie's condition. This time we see Dee agreeing. Allen and Dee discuss how the murder will be carried out. They will hire Mike and Bill again.

We see Dee in Bessie's trailer, telling Bessie that some "roofers" will be there soon to fix her roof. We see Mike and Bill arrive. We see Dee leave. We see the anguish on Dee's face. We know that she has fallen too far to be saved.

We see Dee drunk, sick with self-hatred. She drives to Susan's apartment. She tells Susan about the murders. Susan freaks out, becomes hysterical, says that her mother is a destroyer of lives. Dee tells Susan that she needs her more than ever now. Susan says "I wish you were dead," throws her mother out.

We see Dee and Allen burying the bodies in Venecia's yard.

We see the Venecia house. It is daytime, sunny. Dee and the boys are living there. We see that Cass has gone. Susan shows up with her suitcases. She tells Dee that she will stay by her side. "I hate what you've done, but you're still my mother."

At the dog track we see Allen, Dee, Susan and other friends partying. Allen is a big spender now. We see that Allen is spending too much money. We see that Susan is being crushed under the weight of her knowledge. She is starting to do drugs, drink alcohol. We see that Dee is troubled by the way Susan is following in her mother's footsteps.

In a selling sequence we see that Allen and Dee are selling off Art's property—boat, cars, trailer. Allen poses as ART. With each sale Allen gets the bulk of the money and Dee gets a few hundred bucks. We see that Allen has been taking too much money from the cash register. The franchise licensing corporation is starting to talk about closing the restaurant.

We see Dee and Susan at the restaurant. Dee is running things, Susan is a waitress. A restaurant corporation executive comes in, demanding to see Art Venecia, and asking for the money the restaurant owes. Dee charms the man into waiting another month. Susan is impressed by her mother's performance. Dee is worried about Susan following in her footsteps.

We see things become unraveled: Dee and Susan fight. Susan complains that Allen is getting all the money. "Ma, you should be getting half."

We see Allen railing at the employees because they have been spreading rumors that Art was murdered.

We see the restaurant being closed down because Allen has been stealing all the corporate funds.

We see Allen and Dee selling the Venecia house, with Allen posing as Art Venecia.

We see Dee and Susan, living now in a small, shabby house. Dee is drinking. She is out of work. She is haunted by what she has done. Mother and daughter fight. They make up. Susan is getting ready for work. She remembers something, goes back into the bedroom, slips something into her apron. What is it, Dee asks. Susan stalls. What is it? Susan reveals two nips, small bottles of alcohol that she takes to work. "I need something to get me through the day," she says. It is an echo of something Dee has said earlier in the film. In this moment Dee realizes that the only way to stop Susan's rush to self-destruction is to free her from the guilt of knowing about the crimes.

We see Dee alone. Pacing. Crying. Destroying her liquor bottles.

Susan comes home from work. Dee is sober. She tells Susan to get a pen and paper. Dee begins to dictate her confession. Susan objects. Dee insists that it must be done. As she continues her narrative, looking stronger with each word, we fade out of the flashback and into the prison where Susan and Dee are talking.

We see Susan and Dee discussing the fact that the state attorney wants Susan to testify against her mother. Again, Susan says she will run away to avoid testifying. But Dee tells Susan she must not run away from life. She must do the right thing. She must testify. Dee is finally doing one noble thing: She is giving her daughter permission to testify against her. Mother and daughter hug and kiss and cry together.

We see Susan leave the prison. The first iron door opens for her, then the second, then the door to the parking lot. She is free at last. Words appear on the screen telling us that Dee, Allen, Mike and Bill were all tried for murder and convicted. They are all on Death Row in Florida.

THE END

To learn more about writing for films, you should read Straczynski's book, as well as Syd Field's books, *Screenplay: The Foundations of Scriptwriting*, and *The Screenwriter's Workbook*, both published by Dell.

"Well all that's great, Gary, but I've noticed that not all true crime books get made into films. So what exactly are those movie people looking for?"

I knew you'd ask that, so to get a thorough answer I turned to Todd Harris of Triad Artists. Harris is one of the top agents in Hollywood at selling books to movies.

"If a story is true that's a big plus with producers of television movies," Harris says. "Producers are looking for headline stories. If you've got a story that got a lot of publicity you've got a good shot. They're always looking for stories on hot current issues, like *I Know My First Name is Steven*. And of course they are interested in best-sellers. One of the best things that could happen to a book is that a major star, like a Victoria Principal, takes an interest in it and wants to make a film of it."

Harris notes that there has been a shift recently from producers buying books at the proposal or manuscript stage to buying them after publication, especially if they've sold well.

"If a book is a hardcover it has a much better shot," he says. "There's just more prestige associated with it."

As for what's particularly hard to sell, Harris says, "Books with an unsympathetic central character. You'll see one turned into a film now and then, but it's rare."

Harris notes that every book that comes to an agent is synopsized by the agency, but says that the author can help his case by writing a synopsis or outline "that shows the producer how to solve some of the problems inherent in the book. Show him that it could be a film."

So that's how Todd Harris answers the question he is probably asked most. And here are the five questions I am most often asked about selling books to film, and the answers.

Question: Do you get to say who will star in the film?

Answer: No. I do, however, get to fantasize about who I would like to star in the film.

Question: Do the producers ask you to write the script?

Answer: Not if they can avoid it. Producers prefer to work with established scriptwriters whom they know. If the writer of the book wants to write the script he has to insist on it, and see if the producer is still interested. If the author has not previously written a script that was bought, his best bet is to write a complete script of his book and offer that for sale.

Question: Is it true that they can do pretty much anything they want to your book, and you might not even recognize it when it comes out as a film?

Answer: Yes.

Question: Gary, isn't it true that movie people are money grubbing slime who will lie to you, destroy your artistic vision, and screw you about six different ways?

Answer: I'm sure it is, sometimes. But in my limited experience with movie people I have been treated much better than in my extensive experience with publishing people. The checks have been bigger, and they have arrived on time, which is unheard of in the publishing industry. The movie people I have dealt with have been much more concerned than publishers about what I thought of their handling of my material. So far, I have no complaints.

Question: Gary, are you sure that you have no complaints?

Answer: Okay, that's not quite true. I have no complaints about any of the people who have bought material from me. But one of the slimey things that some producers do is tell your agent that they are interested in your book and might be making an offer. They stall him without actually offering money. Then they crawl around town like cockroaches trying to make a production deal for your book. If they can't make a deal they tell your agent that they've lost interest. In effect they've gotten a free option on the material and made it more difficult for you to sell your book to someone else.

CLOSING WORDS

So now you know everything there is to know about writing a true crime story. Well, not quite. Writing is still an art, not a science, and much of the learning comes in the writing. You will go forth and write stories of your own and perhaps come to situations that I never dreamed of. From your own artistic vision you will create your own solutions. Also, you will read the works of many true crime writers. Study the way they bring real people to life on paper. Listen for the dialogue that sounds as if it is being spoken in the room where you read. Of each paragraph, ask yourself, "Where did the writer get this?" and your guesses, whether they are right or wrong, will be helpful. Do what any wise apprentice does: Study the masters.

So I haven't told you everything; only experience can do that. But, after reading this book, there is one thing you do have for sure. You have the knowledge that there are no great secrets of true crime writing being withheld from you. Most of the researching "technique," as you have seen, is simply a combination of common sense and curiosity. There are no mysterious tricks, membership cards, code words, special credentials or magic writing formulas that separate you from the published true crime writers. The only difference between you and them, if you're a beginner, is that they have studied the craft longer, worked harder at it, and made all those mistakes which comprise the education of any craftsman or artist. You can do the same.

One final note before I leave you, and it concerns one of those craftsman-artists.

I got a letter recently from Joe McGinniss, the author. McGinniss, who has written many different kinds of books, has been outstandingly successful with true crimes. His book, *Fatal Vision*, is one of the classics in the field. It was a best-seller in both hardcover and paperback and it became a network television miniseries. It brought McGinniss money and renewed his fame. More recently McGinniss wrote *Blind Faith*, another true crime book which hit best-seller lists in hardcover and paperback, then became a TV movie. I had asked McGinniss for an interview for this book and he politely declined.

In his letter to me McGinniss made the point that he did not think of himself as a "true crime writer," and he didn't want the public to think of him that way. He is versatile and, in fact, he noted the book he's working on now is about Ted Kennedy. It is not a true crime, nor is the one he plans to write after that.

What has this got to do with you? Quite a bit. It means that the Joe McGinnisses of this world have other fish to fry, and as much as the publishers might want it, these writers are not always going to be working on the true crime books that readers are waiting for. Somebody else will have to write them. It might as well be you.

INDEX

OTHER BOOKS OF INTEREST

Annual Market Books
Novel & Short Story Writer's Market, edited by Robin Gee (paper) $18.95
Photographer's Market, edited by Sam Marshall $21.95
Poet's Market, by Judson Jerome $19.95
Songwriter's Market, edited by Brian Rushing $19.95
Writer's Market, edited by Mark Kissling $24.95

General Writing Books
Beginning Writer's Answer Book, edited by Kirk Polking (paper) $13.95
How to Write a Book Proposal, by Michael Larsen $10.95
Make Your Words Work, by Gary Provost $17.95
On Being a Writer, edited by Bill Strickland $19.95
The 29 Most Common Writing Mistakes & How To Avoid Them, by Judy Delton (paper) $9.95
The Wordwatcher's Guide to Good Writing & Grammar, by Morton S. Freeman (paper) $15.95
Word Processing Secrets for Writers, by Michael A. Banks & Ansen Dibell (paper) $14.95
The Writer's Book of Checklists, by Scott Edelstein $16.95
The Writer's Digest Guide to Manuscript Formats, by Buchman & Groves $17.95

Nonfiction Writing
The Complete Guide to Writing Biographies, by Ted Schwarz $19.95
Creative Conversations: The Writer's Guide to Conducting Interviews, by Michael Schumacher $16.95
How to Sell Every Magazine Article You Write, by Lisa Collier Cool (paper) $11.95
The Magazine Article: How To Think It, Plan It, Write It, by Peter Jacobi $17.95
The Writer's Digest Handbook of Magazine Article Writing, edited by Jean M. Fredette (paper) $11.95

Fiction Writing
Characters & Viewpoint, by Orson Scott Card $13.95
The Complete Guide to Writing Fiction, by Barnaby Conrad $17.95
Creating Characters: How To Build Story People, by Dwight V. Swain $16.95
Dare to Be a Great Writer: 329 Keys to Powerful Fiction, by Leonard Bishop $16.95
Dialogue, by Lewis Turco $13.95
Manuscript Submission, by Scott Edelstein $13.95
Plot, by Ansen Dibell $13.95
Revision, by Kit Reed $13.95
Theme & Strategy, by Ronald B. Tobias $13.95
Writing the Novel: From Plot to Print, by Lawrence Block (paper) $10.95

Special Interest Writing Books
Armed & Dangerous: A Writer's Guide to Weapons, by Michael Newton (paper) $14.95
The Complete Book of Scriptwriting, by J. Michael Straczynski (paper) $11.95
Deadly Doses: A Writer's Guide to Poisons, by Serita Deborah Stevens with Anne Klarner (paper) $16.95
Hillary Waugh's Guide to Mysteries & Mystery Writing, by Hillary Waugh $19.95
How to Write Mysteries, by Shannon OCork $13.95
The Writer's Complete Crime Reference Book, by Martin Roth $19.95
Successful Scriptwriting, by Jurgen Wolff & Kerry Cox (paper) $14.95

The Writing Business
The Complete Guide to Self-Publishing, by Tom & Marilyn Ross (paper) $16.95
The Writer's Friendly Legal Guide, edited by Kirk Polking $16.95
A Writer's Guide to Contract Negotiations, by Richard Balkin (paper) $11.95
The Writer's Guide to Self-Promotion & Publicity, by Elane Feldman $16.95
Writing A to Z, edited by Kirk Polking $22.95

To order directly from the publisher, include $3.00 postage and handling for 1 book and $1.00 for each additional book. Allow 30 days for delivery.

Writer's Digest Books, 1507 Dana Avenue, Cincinnati, Ohio 45207
Credit card orders call TOLL-FREE
1-800-289-0963
Prices subject to change without notice.

Write to this same address for information on *Writer's Digest* magazine, *Story* magazine, Writer's Digest Book Club, Writer's Digest School, and Writer's Digest Criticism Service.